Julius Hawley Seelye

The way, the truth, and the life

lectures to educated Hindus, delivered on his late visit to India

Julius Hawley Seelye

The way, the truth, and the life
lectures to educated Hindus, delivered on his late visit to India

ISBN/EAN: 9783337729097

Printed in Europe, USA, Canada, Australia, Japan

Cover: Foto ©Andreas Hilbeck / pixelio.de

More available books at **www.hansebooks.com**

THE WAY, THE TRUTH, AND THE LIFE.

LECTURES TO EDUCATED HINDUS,

DELIVERED ON HIS LATE VISIT TO INDIA.

BY

Rev. JULIUS H. SEELYE,

PROFESSOR IN AMHERST COLLEGE.

NEW YORK:
ANSON D. F. RANDOLPH & COMPANY,
770 BROADWAY, Cor. 9th St.

INTRODUCTORY NOTE.

THESE lectures are a part of those given before educated Hindus, by Prof. Seelye, on his recent visit to India. The four here published were written out, and issued from the press in Bombay, at the earnest request of native gentlemen, one of whom, an eminent Brahmin scholar, offered to bear the expense of publication. It was a matter of regret that the author's brief stay, and the multiplicity of his engagements, — lecturing, holding personal conferences with inquirers, answering letters received from others, — allowed him time to write out only these; but they will suffice to show the spirit and general character of all.

The interest with which they were received, the large and constantly-increasing audiences of the higher classes, — educated Brahmins, Parsees, and others, — that listened to them, were not more a tribute to the lecturer than an illustration of the power of the truths he presented over their minds and hearts. The interest was eminently suggestive in its relations to the future religious history of India, and was quite beyond the hopes of those who had encouraged the enterprise. The attempt to reach a class hitherto almost wholly neglected, with all their native prejudices against the gospel only intensified by a high intellectual training from which all proper Christian influence had for the most part been rigidly excluded, was indeed an experiment, but one that, whatever might be the issue, was eminently fit to be made, — one worthy the Christian scholar and philanthropist, and one which a missionary body like the American Board might well encourage. The manner of Prof. Seelye's visit was especially favorable, — in no formal connection with any missionary organization, the Christian gentleman travelling at his own charges, delaying a few weeks only in the course of his journey before returning to his professional labors, and staying longer than his personal convenience permitted, because he could not refuse the earnest requests to continue his lectures as long as possible, — he had a rare vantage-ground, which he knew how to turn to good account. Yet the secret of his success lay yet more in the fundamental truths of the gospel which he pressed with so much clearness and force upon the *moral nature* of his hearers, commending himself to every man's conscience in the sight of God.

INTRODUCTORY NOTE.

The attention given these lectures at Bombay and Poona, is a striking illustration of the oneness of the moral sentiment amid the most diverse races of men.

They are reprinted, and given to the American public, not simply to gratify a worthy curiosity on the part of many who have felt an interest in the success of Prof. Seelye's efforts, but as an earnest presentation of first principles in morals and religion that will be welcomed by thoughtful men, especially by students in our literary institutions.

Prof. Seelye found in circulation among English readers in India, a printed lecture of his on miracles, originally given as a part of a course * by different gentlemen in Boston. It has been thought wise to publish it with the others, that the volume may find a larger audience, and, it is to be hoped, to make his visit yet more effective for good. The subject-matter of the lecture thus added, and the discussion it receives, render its appearance here especially appropriate.

N. G. CLARK.

CONGREGATIONAL HOUSE,
  BOSTON, Aug, 14, 1873.

* Boston Lectures, 1870.

PREFACE TO THE BOMBAY EDITION.

During the present season, Prof. Seelye, visiting Bombay on a journey around the world, was invited to remain, and give some religious addresses to the educated natives. He was heard attentively by large and intelligent audiences, among whom a strong desire was expressed that the addresses might be published. They had not, however, been previously written; but Prof. Seelye was induced to prepare, according to his recollection, the first four, which are herewith presented, in the hope that they may further the object for which they were given.

GEO. BOWEN.

Bombay, February, 1873.

I.

THE DESIRABLE END OF PROGRESS.

Gentlemen, — All the chief nations of the world just now seem passing through a period of extraordinary changes. In my own land, we have lately experienced the most momentous movement since our history began. You are perhaps familiar with its outlines. A struggle of opinion respecting human slavery grew into a conflict of arms, terribly vast, which has ended both in the overthrow of slavery and in its perpetual prohibition. Passing westward, we find unprecedented changes taking place in Japan. It is scarcely ten years since the first Japanese student came, for an education, to the United States; but such was the opposition then to any intercourse with the outside world, that he was obliged to leave his country by stealth, and would have lost his head had he been discovered. Japan was then a feudal State, without a code of laws, having an arbitrary despot at its head, and a host of petty princes owing him subjection, but wielding also a tyrannical power over their own territories and retainers. Within ten years this has all been changed. Japan has now a constitutional monarch, with an official cabinet and parliament; and the feudal princes have yielded up their rank, while nine-tenths of their former revenue goes to the support of the new order of things. Two hundred Japanese students, sent and supported by the government itself, are now pursuing their education in the United States; while others also, under the same auspices, are in England and the Continental States of Europe. China, though holding fast her traditional dislike — a mingled hatred and contempt — of foreigners and their ways, finds it impossible to preserve her isolation; and the Chinese government has the present year sent to the United States thirty young men, to pursue there a course of study for a term of fifteen years, and has also decreed that a similar number, for a similar course, should follow them during each of the next ensuing four years. You know the changes, and their vast significance, which have recently occurred, and are still transpiring, in European nations; while in India it requires no close observer to discover underlying tendencies of thought and action indicative of momentous movements among yourselves.

Looking over the whole field, and bringing the nations into one view, it would be interesting to inquire whether all these currents, comprehensively examined, can be seen to set in any one direction, which might indicate the actual goal of human progress. But there is another inquiry, preliminary to that: What is the most desirable goal? What sort of progress for mankind will be sought by the wisest well-wisher of his race?

To this question various answers can be given, only one of which can be true. Advancement in what may be termed the material arts of civilization is sometimes claimed to be the most desirable sort of progress. Let man subdue nature, it is said. Let there be a great increase of railroads and telegraph lines, and useful inventions of all sorts. Multiply manufactures, and increase commerce, and let the means of satisfying human wants grow as the wants themselves enlarge: thus you will strengthen men's sense of dependence upon each other, wars will cease, nations will be bound together in a brotherhood of common interest, and, in this advancing growth, the highest advance of civilization is to be reached. Thus we often hear.

But there are two difficulties with all this, which we may not wisely ignore. The first is, that these arts of material progress have no power of reproduction. They cannot perpetuate themselves. There are instances innumerable where these arts, with no power other than their own to sustain them, have been left to die and disappear. Where are the arts which built the Great Pyramid, apparently the oldest monument of human workmanship now existing? The Astronomer Royal of Scotland, who has spent months in its careful measurements and study, aided by the best instruments which London and Paris and Vienna could supply, declares that the builders of this structure must have had instruments exceeding in accuracy his own. You have perhaps seen statements of recent researches in your neighboring kingdom of Cambodia, where ruins of extensive dwellings of elaborate workmanship appear, built long ago by the ancestors of men who now live in the tops of trees, to escape from tigers. The exquisite bronzes and lacquer-work made in earlier times in Japan, the Japanese cannot now equal; while the beautiful colors which the Chinese formerly exhibited in their porcelains, and the bronzes inlaid with silver which they formerly wrought so perfectly, they cannot now produce. In the ruins of Philæ and Karnak and ancient Thebes, in Nineveh and Balbec, in Yucatan and Mexico, are evidences abundant of arts once possessed, but long since lost, because their possessors had nothing but the arts themselves with which to preserve them. It is a great mistake, based upon a very superficial philosophy, and resting on a science falsely so called, which supposes that there naturally exists in human society an inherent power of progress, capable, through its own evolution, of perpetual growth. The deepest principles of human nature, and all the facts of history, declare exactly the reverse. We pride ourselves upon our useful arts, upon the triumphs of the industry and invention of the present time, and there are enough who fancy these to be the all-sufficient good; but, if we seek to perpetuate these by their own power alone, can any one tell why they should not ultimately disappear and perish, as has been done in so many instances before? We do not avoid the force of this by saying, that, if some arts disappear, others arise whose sum equals or exceeds in value those lost; for why do they arise? Out of what source does the impulse to all this advancement actually spring? Our material wants do not give birth to our material progress;

rather does the progress itself evoke and enlarge, and first make us conscious of our wants. The luxuries of one age have been called the necessities of another. It is not the wants of the savage — his need of food and shelter — which start him on the track of civilization; for we find these wants among vast multitudes of men without the faintest gleam of progress. As a matter of fact, we always find that it is some spiritual impulse which impels men in their material progress; and, unless this impulse is furnished and kept alive, neither can arts be preserved, nor, if lost, can they be restored.

The other difficulty is thus indicated. This material advancement can in no respect create that spiritual impulse, of which it is altogether the creature. The mental progress, of which it is the sign and fruit, finds in it no sufficient stimulus nor food, and, with nothing else to support it, becomes exhausted. Moreover, as all experience shows, the union of men in material interest is helpless in securing their true or lasting fellowship. The so-called arts of peace have, by themselves, no power of averting war. The history of the last ten years in Europe and America shows that the closest ties of blood and common interest offer no restraint to people whom other influences set on strife. A few years ago it was said in the United States that no conflict of arms between the North and South need be apprehended, because, besides our kinship, there were our railroads and telegraphs and postal communications, and the myriad interdependences of trade, to bind us indissolubly together; but, when the thoughts and sentiments of the two sections became irreconcilable, all these material bonds were but as the seven green withs upon the strong man, which he brake with his strength, "even as a thread of tow is broken when it toucheth the fire." Bands of steel are fragile as threads of gossamer in the presence of ideas, and under the power of spiritual principles. The desirable goal of civilization, therefore, cannot be reached by any material progress.

Shall we seek it, then, in something intellectual? Will education furnish us the true good? There are men enough who ask if ignorance be not the source of all our trouble, for which knowledge is the only and all-sufficient relief. Educate men therefore! Open the gateways of science, and bid the human race ascend on the broad paths of knowledge to its high goal! Of course, nothing need be said against education, in itself considered; only ignorance despises knowledge: but, when we set before us for attainment the true and highest good for men, there are certain difficulties in our way, which no amount of knowledge or of culture can possibly remove. I will not dwell upon the fact, shown by manifold illustrations, that culture has no more power to perpetuate itself than has the material progress we have just considered. History is full of instances where sciences and arts and literatures and civilizations have declined. But, besides this, growth in knowledge, or culture of the intellect, cannot be man's highest good; for, since this can only be secured in the highest degree by the most exclusive devotion to its pursuit, it must, from the nature of the case, be confined to a few, and can never be enjoyed by the great mass of mankind. The necessities of human life have always required, as they must ever do, on the part of most men, vastly other occupations than those which the cultivated man must follow, if he pursues his culture, while the true good should be one which all men might attain. That good, which, from its nature, can only be given to a small portion of the race, is not wisely to be proposed as the most desirable end of human progress.

But a graver difficulty remains. You will acknowledge that there is no satisfactory condition of human life without virtue, — that a social state lacking in integrity and purity could be no proper model for imitation, whatever its degree of culture or material progress. No good can remain untainted in the midst of a prevailing moral defilement. "No nation," said the great historian Niebuhr, "ever died except by suicide;" and the suicidal poison is always engendered by the nation's moral corruption. Now, I affirm, and if you will note closely the facts in the case you will not doubt the statement, that culture fails in the highest requirement here; for it is powerless to secure virtue, or to interpose any efficient obstacle against vice. I might prove this from the universal principles of human nature; but this is unnecessary, since it is declared, with such startling clearness, by the facts of history. Conspicuous examples abound of the failure of culture to produce any moral improvement of men, or to resist the destructive influence of a corrupt society. Take ancient Athens. Perhaps no people ever attained so refined or exalted a culture as the Athenians possessed during the time of Pericles, — a culture so wide-reaching that even the common people were students of philosophy and accomplished critics of art. In no city, surely, of the present day, would an artist think of asking or abiding by the judgment of the common people upon his productions; but this was a matter of every-day occurrence at Athens. Not only smiths, tanners, and cobblers, as Xenophon expresses it, gathered together to hear the discussions of philosophers, but the same classes came from their homes and their workshops to the market-place, and pronounced their verdict upon the highest works of art ever submitted to any age; and their verdict has been respected by every age. But all this surprising culture, unparalleled in its perfection, left the soul of the people dead. It showed not the slightest power to purify. It brought forth no virtue, and checked no vice. The evidence of Athenian corruption in the most blooming period of Athenian culture is overwhelming and appalling. A strong argument might be constructed to show that this enlightened centre of art and philosophy was the most corrupt city of its time. In one of Plato's dialogues, an intimate friend and pupil of Socrates extols his master in a eulogium which has been even called an apotheosis, wherein it is put forth, as a matter equally of wonder and of admiration, that Socrates alone, one single man in all Athens, was not guilty of a vice too revolting to be named! The whole atmosphere of Athens was surcharged with a moral pestilence, whose ravages were most dire, even when the results of culture were the most splendid. The culture, unable to resist the moral corruption, itself yielded and fell before it, till the cradle of art and philosophy became also its grave. Such a fact — to which your own familiarity, gentlemen, with the records of history will suggest copious parallels drawn from individuals and communities — teaches us, that, unless we have some end to attain higher than culture, and some instrument more potent than culture to employ, all our hopes of human progress and of the highest civilization are in vain.

Shall we seek, then, this higher end and more potent instrument in virtue itself? Granted that no result would be satisfactory in which moral purity does not reign, shall we endeavor to secure this purity by instructing men in its precepts? Alas, gentlemen, if you closely judge, either from human nature or from history, you will predict the inevitable failure of all such attempts. Instruction in moral precepts gives no inspiration to virtue, as facts abundantly show. We are liable to a great mistake here, — a mistake actually made by many men, who, from a false theory of human nature, draw conclusions which all the facts of human conduct deny. It is judged, that, because men ought to act virtuously, they would do so if they could only see this duty with unmistakable clearness; but the simple fact is, that they do see it, and have always seen it. No man needs to be told that he ought to do right: he knows it without any telling; and oh, how feeble are all the instructions of another, in comparison with the strength and the majesty of that undying voice, which, in every man's soul, has been proclaiming his duty ever since he had a soul! The great trouble is, that men will not do their duty when it is known; and how shall any increasing instruction reach or remedy this?

Socrates furnishes a conspicuous example of the failure of this method. Of all the world's great ethical teachers, no one seems to have had as complete a conviction as he, that instruction in virtue is sufficient to secure virtue. Virtue is teachable, was his famous motto, on the basis of which he went about for thirty years, through the streets and workshops of Athens, illustrating and expounding his favorite theme, seeking ever to make men virtuous by instructing them in the precepts of virtue. Does any one doubt the matchless skill with which this great master inculcated his lessons? Is any one likely to exaggerate the prodigious intellectual results of his teaching? These abide still, and are certain to far outlast our time; but we have no evidence of the slightest moral improvement resulting from all the efforts of Socrates. Alcibiades, one of his most intimate and attentive pupils and friends, upon whom Socrates exerted all his power of reformation, remained a licentious and hopeless profligate; and it does not appear, that, in any instance, this master of spiritual births, as he termed himself, was able to bring forth one virtuous impulse to a virtuous life. In all this, Socrates only illustrates the universal law. No preaching of morality, unattended by any other influence, has ever sunk deep into society, or spread widely in the thoughts and actions of men. It has never shown any power to mould society internally and from the centre. It is a very narrow reading of history, and a very shallow acquaintance with the heart, which has not yet taught us that something other than knowledge is necessary in order to virtue, that something more than light is needed in order to life.

But if instruction in virtue were all-sufficient to secure virtuous conduct, yet if we look more profoundly into such conduct, good and desirable as it is, we shall not find it the highest object of a wise man's desire. For this conception of virtue never rises higher than the thought of duty — the thought of something which ought to be done. It commands, it prohibits, and we fulfil its mandates when we do what it bids us do. But there is a great difference between doing righteously and being righteous, — between obedience to a law and the inspiration of a life. The constraint of moral precept can, at the best, only mould our deeds: it cannot shape our inclinations, nor furnish any inner and living spring to moral action. You may teach a blind man how to direct his steps, and by some leading string he may follow your directions perfectly; but oh, how much better when he has his own eye, and walks in the light of his own clear seeing! You may make a marble statue, faultless in its beauty; but how much better that breathing creation which God has made, which is instinct with life, and which moves as its free spirit guides it! And thus, however perfectly you may regulate your conduct by the constraint of duty, it is a far higher and nobler life, when your spirit needs no external constraint to control it, but chooses truth and righteousness in the exercise of its perfect liberty and because of its perfect love. A fountain of purity opened in the depth and centre of the soul, and fed exhaustlessly with the spontaneous impulse of life, every one who intelligently seeks, either his own good or the highest welfare of society, will surely desire; but this perfect life is inconceivable, apart from a divine quickening, and demands a religious source alike to evoke and sustain it. Religion has, therefore, in all time and by the great majority of men, been felt to be indispensable to the highest good. No material prosperity, nor culture, nor virtue, however extended, refined, or sure, can adequately bless men.

There are two kinds of religion, and only two. The one begins with man, and seeks, by human endeavors, after a divine fellowship. It has various forms, — Paganism in all its branches, Mohammedanism, besides various representatives in nominal Christian lands; but the one characteristic in which they are all united is that they seek after God in some way which the human intellect has been able to devise, and by some practices which the human will is able to perform. The God whom they seek may be called the Absolute, or Infinite, or Allah, or Buddha, or Brahm; he may be dimly apprehended, or worshipped as altogether unknown; he may dwell in some high heavens above us, or, as we are sometimes told, in some deep heavens within; but whatsoever he may be called, or whatsoever he may be, the human soul, perhaps by penance, perhaps by prayer, perhaps by calm and rapt contemplation, seeks if haply it might feel after and find him. In this point Paganism and Pantheism, the rudest systems of untutored thought and the refined speculations of acute and cultured minds, meet and agree. The spectacle which these religions furnish is certainly most impressive. Whatever we may say of the forms in which the religious sentiment has been exhibited, no one can smile, none can sneer, at the sentiment itself.

But what have all these efforts of man to find some religion accomplished? Taking them all together, they have never furnished any deathless impulse to society nor any undying inspiration to the soul: they have made men sometimes calm with a stoical indifference, and sometimes mute with a hopeless despair; but they have never checked nor changed the tendency of the evil they were designed to destroy, while the mysterious instinct, the importunate craving, out of which the religion has its birth, the religion itself is equally unable to stifle or to satisfy.

I said there are two kinds of religion, and only two. The one begins with man, and seeks, by human endeavors, after God; the other begins with God, and, by a way wholly divine, seeks after man. In this is the peculiarity of the Christian, in distinction from all other systems of religion; and, in the revelation of this doctrine, is the distinction of the Bible from all other books.

I remember, in one of the Hymns of the Rig Veda, a single expression like this: "He is merciful even to him that committeth sin." There is some uncertainty about the proper interpretation of the passage; but, granting that here is a thought which sounds like the characteristic doctrine of the Christian Scriptures, I know of nothing similar to it, elsewhere, in the records of the unchristian world. While the thought of God's justice is universal, and the idea of propitiation is everywhere found, only in the Bible is the divine justice radiant with love, and the sacrifice, on whose meritorious ground rests the forgiveness of sins, represented as altogether the work of God himself. But this doctrine, which the Christian system was the first to declare, reigns through every portion of that system. The salvation which the Christian religion announces is procured wholly through a divine work, and is offered to man, not in the least because his obedience or service can merit it, but solely through the free exercise of divine mercy. It comes to men, first of all, in their disobedience, when ruined by sin, and offers them forgiveness and life as a free gift. The Christian Scriptures expressly declare that "God commendeth his love to us, in that while we were yet sinners Christ died for us;" that Christ came "to seek and to save that which was lost;" and that, "not by works of righteousness which we have done, but by his mercy he saved us."

Notice now the living inspiration which this truth gives to men. God's love to man, thus revealed, begets man's love to God; for "we love him because he first loved us;" and man's love to God kindles man's love to man, "for he that loveth God will love his brother also." This living germ is capable of evolving the perfect life for the individual, and the perfect social state. All the requirements of individual perfection are met in that soul where every duty and every moral precept are revealed as the righteous will of a loving Lord, in whose love the soul finds its life, and in whose service it rejoices in the liberty of the perfect love which casteth out fear. The perfect social state surely exists when society, kindled by this divine inspiration, becomes knit together by that charity which seeketh not her own, and where the new life of love and purity in individual hearts works everywhere in peace and good-will. These blessings, which no other religion even proposes, and which surpass the ideal dreams of poetry or philosophy, it is not only the actual aim of Christianity to secure, but these are the actual results of this religion, in exactly the degree in which men have yielded to its sway. If it could only be everywhere accepted, if all men were true and loyal disciples of Jesus Christ, wars would cease, oppression and slavery would be no more, vice and crime of every sort would disappear; there would be purity and love universal among men, and the spiritual life which the Christian faith enkindles would furnish the unfailing impulse to all intellectual growth and all industrial activity. Not only righteousness, but knowledge, should then flow through all the earth, while the wilderness and the solitary place should be glad thereof, and the desert should rejoice and blossom as the rose. The wise man, therefore, who loves his race, will be content with nothing less than the effort to bring all nations and every heart under the living sway of Jesus Christ and his word.

II.

THE CHRISTIAN RELIGION WORTHY OF EXAMINATION.

GENTLEMEN, — It is related in the New Testament that Philip, one of the earliest disciples of Christ, went to a friend, Nathanael by name, and said, "We have found him of whom Moses in the Law, and the Prophets, did write, Jesus of Nazareth, the son of Joseph." Now, both the Law and the Prophets had foretold that the Messiah who was to come should descend from David, and be born at Bethlehem. Nathanael perfectly understood this, and therefore put no faith in Philip's statement. With no attempt to explain its seeming discrepancy from all he had been taught to believe, with no inquiry whether Jesus of Nazareth might not have been born at Bethlehem, and the reputed son of Joseph be of the real lineage of David, he embodies his sceptical objections in the scornful reply, "Can there any good thing come out of

Nazareth?" Philip makes no reply to the objection by way of formal argument, but simply invites Nathanael to come and see for himself. His words, in substance, were, This is all true which I tell you. Jesus of Nazareth, the son of Joseph, is the Messiah; and, if you will but come and see him as I have done, and know him as I do, your doubts will disappear, and your faith will be as firm as mine. Nathanael consents. He goes. He finds Jesus. He hears his words. He becomes acquainted with his character. His examination satisfies him, and he believes. "Rabbi," he exclaims, "thou art the Son of God, thou art the King of Israel."

I refer to this incident, because it illustrates two facts often found. When the claims of the Christian religion are presented, they may seem to contradict some preconceived opinion, and are therefore scornfully set aside. One who has tested these claims himself, however, and knows their power, will not hesitate to challenge any objector to come and see for himself. Christianity has nothing to conceal from friend or foe.

It is not only open for the examination of the world, but it challenges the closest scrutiny, and is not afraid of the result. Try me, it says to all the opposing thoughts and systems of men. Examine my claims in whatever aspect and by whatever test you please; the highest flights of human thought, the profoundest research, and the widest range of inquiry, shall find me higher, broader, and deeper than they have reached.

This claim of the Christian religion for examination is supported by considerations so numerous and weighty, that I beg to press it upon your attention. It is not my present purpose to enter upon any formal presentation of the evidences of Christianity, but only to refer you to some of the more obvious and most indisputable grounds upon which this religion claims the thoughtful scrutiny of the world.

1. The Christian religion is a fact in the world, and must have originated in some way. And now there is the clearest certainty that it was first known among men a little more than eighteen hundred years ago, and that its author was an individual who bore the name of Jesus. This certainty has been established after so searching a scrutiny, and in the face of so strong an opposition, that it may be regarded as a fact undisputed and indisputable. But more than this is true. The general points in the narrative of the New Testament are now past contradiction. One would not add to his reputation for intelligence who should doubt or deny that Soc-

rates taught men in the streets of Athens, or that Plato held his profound discussions in the Academy, or that Aristotle walked to and fro amid the shady groves of the lyceum discoursing with his disciples. Those persons who are anxious to be called independent thinkers would be called very independent indeed to dispute such points as these. And yet none of these are better authenticated than the general facts of the gospel history. This history has been subjected to a criticism of unparalleled rigor and learning; but it has stood the searching ordeal, and has come forth from the furnace as gold tried in the fire. By far the ablest work which the present century has produced against the acceptation in which the New Testament is commonly held by Christians, the work which shows greater learning, and more philosophical power, than almost any other, on that side of the question, — I refer of course to Strauss's "Life of Jesus," — admits that the large basis of historical truth in the Gospels can no longer be denied. The more brilliant, though far less profound, work of Rénan, recently attracting an attention which it has already lost, re-affirms this admission as positively as the most confident believer in Christianity could desire. There are questions still at issue respecting particular points in the gospel narratives, — questions which advancing discussion is steadily bringing to an issue more and more accordant with the views of Christian believers;* but no question any longer exists respecting their general truthfulness. We may take it, therefore, as a fact no more to be denied, that Jesus Christ actually lived and died, in all general respects, as the New Testament says he did.

Notice some of these facts. He belonged to the humblest rank in society. His reputed father was a carpenter. His mother was so poor that she could bring to the temple only a pair of turtle-doves, or two young pigeons, — the gift of the poorest (Lev. xii. 8, Luke ii. 24) as her offering after his birth. Till he was thirty years of age, Jesus lived with his parents, poor, unnoticed, unknown. He had no rich and powerful friends, nor any external means of influence. No patronage was shown him, no earthly master gave him instruction. It is comparatively easy to gain favor and credence for a system, where the rich, the learned, the noble

---

* The strongest objections to the New Testament have lately been urged to its miracles, which are declared to be impossible on scientific grounds; but the recent remarkable mathematical demonstrations, which Clausius has applied to the mechanical theory of heat, prove not only the entire possibility of miracles, on scientific grounds, but their absolute necessity to account for the present condition of things.

support it: Christ had none of these on his side; but they were all leagued against him. It was no impossible thing for Mohammed to conquer nations with the sword; but Christ commenced his mission, and finished it, preaching peace. If his nation had been expecting the advent of such a person as he, it would not have been difficult to impose upon such expectations; but the Jews were looking for the coming of a very different Messiah; and there was that in the appearance of Jesus which made his claims to be the Anointed of God the greatest absurdity in their eyes: "Can there any good thing come out of Nazareth?" "Is not this the carpenter's son?" And yet, with every thing to contend with, and nothing to help him but himself, and even his own rank and condition all apparently against him, this poor, unlettered, and obscure individual, at thirty years of age calmly presented himself to his nation and to the world as their divine Teacher and Saviour and Lord. Never before or since has any other man, whatever his power, uttered such pretensions. The dreams of insanity do not surpass it; but the dignity and calmness and self-possession of Jesus are as unparalleled as his claims. His whole conduct shows that he knew himself, and had the clearest consciousness of what he said and did.

He always continued poor. He never sought wealth, nor applause, nor any other power than his own. Without even a place which he could call his own, where he could lay his head, despised and rejected by the ruling classes, finding his companions among the destitute and the outcasts of society, he spent three years, teaching and preaching the kingdom of God. They were years of bitter toil and hardship; but he never complained, he never sought his own ease, nor excused himself from any work for another's good. At the end of three years he was put to an ignominious death; and yet this poor, despised, and crucified person has been loved and served and worshipped ever since, by increasing multitudes, who, somehow or other, have come to feel that all their hopes for this life and the life to come centre in him. The most interesting question, in the most enlightened portion of the world, exerting a wider attention and more earnest thought to-day than any other theme, relates to the person and work of one, who, eighteen hundred years ago, was ignominiously put to death as a malefactor. How do you account for this? It is, to say the least, the most striking phenomenon in history: what is its explanation? Come and see. A wise man will not rest till he has solved, if he can, such a problem as this.

2. Whatever may be said of the Christian religion, it must certainly be confessed, that, from an origin so humble, there have sprung effects incalculably exalted. The crucifixion of Christ was an event which both astonished and terrified the few, who, during his life, adhered to him. All their fondest hopes were destroyed by his death. Why were not the disciples themselves disheartened and dispersed? Doubtless this is what every one beforehand would have predicted. The disciples were a little band of rude, and illiterate men. They were destitute, in all respects, of what the world calls power. They had no remarkable gifts of reason or of speech. They could wield neither the pen, the purse, nor the sword. Not only were they the weakest instruments, and their means the feeblest, but the work of preaching the new religion demanded the strongest agencies in the hands of the strongest men. If they were to go forward and preach the doctrine of their Master, from how many sources might they not expect a most bitter opposition! Every government and army, every school of learning, the literatures and arts of the world, the institutions of society, and the deep-seated tendencies of the soul, would be all leagued against them. What could they do? What did they do? They opened

their mouths boldly, and ceased not to teach and to preach that Jesus is the Christ. They went everywhere, declaring that this Jesus, who was crucified, is the Lord and Saviour of mankind. They were able — these few poor and illiterate followers of a despised and crucified Master were able — to convince others that their statements were true. The Roman Empire, the mightiest the world has known, made every effort to suppress the new faith, but the faith grew notwithstanding, till it took possession of the very power which had been set for its destruction. How could this be? The astonishing fact demands an explanation.

In only two other instances do we know the history of the propagation of a new system of religion; but the problem which the rise and spread of Mohammedanism or of Buddhism present is very simple in comparison with that which belongs to the early extension of Christianity. The triumphs of Mohammedanism were gained, as you well know, by physical force. The ascendency of the Koran, in every nation which accepted it, was accomplished by the sword. In the case of Buddhism, the abandonment by the great Shakya-Muni of his princely rank and inheritance, and his devotion to a life of poverty and asceticism, was a most impressive spectacle; and the vigor with which, for so many years, he preached his doctrine of the vanity of earthly things, could not fail to draw around him a multitude of weary and wretched souls, to whom relief from the misery of a hopeless existence was welcome at any price, even that of existence itself. But you are acquainted with the fact that Buddhism gained no strong foothold, and maintained only a precarious existence, until, two hundred years after the death of its founder, Chandragupta, or Sandracottas as he is called in the Western world, gave it his patronage, thinking that he could thus strengthen his throne against the hostile influence of Brahminism; while it was only through the power of Chandragupta's grandson, Asoka, who conquered so large a portion of India, that Buddhism became a dominant religion in this land. You know, too, that when this faith spread into the regions where it still reigns, it was carried first of all through the agencies of political power, and that it gained no footing in any land except as it adopted and wove into its own system the superstitions already existing there. But I need not tell you the difference between all this and the early spread of the Christian gospel. Christianity had no armies, but it conquered armies. It started with an obscure individual of mean parentage, in a despised city of a narrow province of the Roman Empire, and was without the slightest semblance of political power; but the strongest government of the world came to acknowledge its supremacy. It entered into no compromise with other systems of religion; but it simply overthrew them, and took their place in the ascendency they had held. It never yielded a whit to human passions. It was at war with all pride and selfishness and sensuality; but it conquered human hearts, and changed them according to its will. The introduction and early spread of Christianity are facts without a parallel, and can be accounted for by none of the ordinary principles which explain the conduct of men.

But the subsequent history of Christianity is no less marvellous. It met and subdued the barbarous hordes who overran Europe and broke up the Roman Empire, and, by its simple power, has raised them to a height of social prosperity never known before. It has entered, with a fresh and living inspiration, into all the art and culture which have succeeded its introduction. It has given life to every genuine reform, and has proved itself to be the only agency which has ever shown itself able truly to educate and elevate the world.

Much is said, in our day, about freedom; but the world's knowledge and possession of liberty are coincident with the rise and progress of Christ's kingdom. The very idea of liberty was wanting to men till it was made clear by the Christian doctrine. There was no knowledge of freedom in all this Oriental world. Take India as an illustration, and find, if you can, in the dreams of your poets, or the sayings of your philosophers, or the doctrines of your religion, any more than in the practices of the governments which early reigned here, a recognition of the thought that man is entitled to freedom. You know very well that there was no liberty here; that the only person who was called free was a despot, and he was not a free man. The same was true elsewhere. We sometimes talk of the notion of liberty as held by the ancient Greeks and Romans; but this notion differs radically from that which men have since received from the Christian doctrine. All that the Greeks and Romans knew of liberty was liberty for a class, — liberty for a few, and not for all mankind. The Athenian knew that he himself was free, and the native Roman citizen knew that he was free born; but that it constituted the true and proper being of all men to be free, that man as man is free born, this knew neither Plato nor Aristotle, neither

Cicero nor the teacher of Roman law. In the great Christian principle that Christ is the Son of God, and that he died for man, is contained the thought that the individual soul, which has cost such a redemption, is of infinite worth, — a thought in whose light differences of rank disappear, and all men, Greek and Barbarian, Jew and Gentile, bond and free, are seen to stand on equal terms before God. The blessings which men have actually received from this doctrine of liberty have been in exact proportion to the clearness with which the Christian thought which contains it has been apprehended. The Christian doctrine that salvation is not acquired by our own works, and does not depend upon any rank or righteousness or merit of men, but is wrought out for us and within us by Christ's all-perfect work, and is received, in God's free grace, through a simple faith in what Christ has done, — this doctrine was set before the world as the true doctrine of the Christian Scriptures, in the great Reformation of the sixteenth century, with such a clearness and power that it has been followed, in the three hundred years succeeding, by a wider extension of liberty, and a further increase of political and social blessings, among those who have accepted the Reformation, than had been attained by all the world in all its history before. Nor let any one fancy that this is an accidental connection, or one only of time and space; for every close student will see the causal link which binds these facts together. "The doctrine of Justification by Faith," says Sir James Mackintosh, "is the basis of civil freedom." Hume declares, and no intelligent person will doubt, that it is to the preaching of the Puritans, who were a true product of the Reformation, that England owes her civil liberties. The movement for the destruction of the slave-trade and the abolition of slavery sprang from the same source. Sir Fowell Buxton, who made the first motion in the English Parliament for the abolition of slavery in the British West Indies, has left on record that his first impulse to this course was due to the Christian preaching in the chapel he was wont to attend. The movement, bitterly opposed by selfishness and cupidity, was carried to a successful issue by those who believed that Christ has died for all men, and therefore that all have a right to freedom. It is the same belief, which would not yield even in the face of arms, which has carried forward the recent struggle in the United States to the entire and perpetual abolition of slavery there. Slavery has ceased in every Protestant country, not because governments have conceded freedom as a privilege, but because men have claimed it as a right; but the right has never been seen and never maintained except as the Christian doctrine has first revealed it to men, and then inspired them with the hope of its possession.

Christianity has not only shown itself sufficient to reform political institutions and improve the social condition of men, but it has wrought religious changes still more extensive. It is the only religion which has ever been able effectually to root out and supplant another. To a certain degree we find in different nations different systems of religion, each of which expresses some national trait, and represents a certain phase of national development. Resting so firmly in national peculiarities, they hold a strong ground, from which they are only with extreme difficulty dislodged. And, as a matter of fact, no power has been able to overcome this difficulty except that of the Christian religion alone. In other instances where two religions have come in contact, the result has been either their amalgamation, or the temporary yielding of the one to the other by the constraint of physical power. You know how that Buddhism in India overbore and crowded down for a time the prevailing Brahminism, which, however, it did not destroy; but which showed itself able, when the opportunity came, to throw aside the later faith, and regain its old ascendency. There is no longer any Buddhism in the land of its earliest and extensive triumphs; while it maintains itself among the millions where it is found in other lands only in so far as it has availed itself of forces not originally its own. Christianity is the only religion, which, by the simple might of its own principles, has ever truly taken the place of another. And can it have done this, unless it has something which penetrates deeper susceptibilities of the soul than are reached by the feelings of a race, or the thoughts of a nation?

And whatever this religion has done has been always in face of an intense opposition. Its victories, unparalleled and mighty as they are, have never been achieved without a struggle. There have always been unbelievers outside the Church, who have found fault with its evidences and rejected its claims. There have sometimes also been found men within the church content to receive the emoluments and dignities of high ecclesiastical office, while they have despised the doctrines and derided the faith they were expected to teach. I enter here into no criticism upon their conduct, and only allude to it to make clear the fact that all the hold of the Christian system, now or in the past, on the thoughts of men, has been obtained by a triumph of its principles through a sore conflict with opposing thoughts. Moreover, this conflict of thought but partly represents that deeper hostility of sentiment and will which this religion necessarily excites in every breast. It is not only a form of doctrine, but it demands a changed purpose and a new life from all who receive it. The words of Jesus to his original disciples are the only terms in which his claims can be presented: "If any man will come after me, let him deny himself, and take up his cross, and follow me" (Matt. xvi. 24). "He that loveth father or mother more than me is not worthy of me; and he that loveth son or daughter more than me is not worthy of me. And he that taketh not his cross and followeth after me is not worthy of me" (Matt. x. 37, 38).

In this continued struggle with the thoughts and sentiments and will of men, the Christian religion has been continuously victorious. No one can study its history without noting that apparent reverses have revealed themselves, in the course of time, to have been genuine steps of progress; and no one can study the history of the world without noting that its only line of unfading light and growing splendor is that traversed by the progress of the Christian faith. I know, that, in Christian lands, there are evils still unsubdued which Christianity aims to destroy; but the undoubted fact remains of their steady diminution before the steady growth of Christian influence. By the ancestors of the present Christian nations, war was recognized as a nation's normal state, and the same word designated a foreigner and a foe; but surely all this has changed, and the feeling grows in Christian lands that nations should live together in peace. In confirmation of this remark, I point to the way in which, during the present year, two of the most prominent Christian nations have settled a grave international dispute. England and the United States agreed to refer to arbitration a matter which formerly they would have sought to settle with the sword; and that this agreement has been secured by a growth, in both these nations, of the Christian sentiment respecting war and national friendship, will not be denied. Christianity seeks the overthrow of all evil among men. Its grand aim, which it unceasingly puts forth, is to remove all war and oppression, and vice and crime, to elevate and ennoble and purify all the relations of man to his fellow-man, and to bind all nations together in the organic unity of a body wherein Christian love is the in-dwelling soul, and Christ himself the ever-living head. To its power of accomplishing all this, the Christian religion fearlessly challenges every scrutiny. It points to its principles, and to what it has already done, as the evidence of its aim, and of what it can do. Slowly, indeed, but none the less steadily and mightily, is its great work moving on. Notwithstanding the difficulties ever in its path, it holds a stronger power in the world to-day than it has ever done before. From the icy north, from the sunny south, from the far-off isles of the sea, from the roving tribes of the desert, from the savage wanderers of the forest, from the cultivated circles of enlightened life, from city and from hamlet, from rich and poor, from learned and ignorant men, from every class and clime, there come the trophies of its victorious power. Look at the influence of the Christian religion as it now actually exists, and tell me what this marvel means, if that which causes it be not of God.

3. Pass now from these general considerations, and see what this religion does for the individual character. It aims to change and reform men; which it also has certainly done, in unnumbered instances. It has entered the heart, and tamed fierce passions, and transformed obstinate prejudices, and rooted out deep-seated desires, and given new hopes, a new purpose, and a new life; and it offers to do this in behalf

of every one who will follow its precepts. Look, in illustration of its power, at the changes which it wrought in such a man as Saul of Tarsus. No one can doubt the general historical accuracy of the narrative respecting him as given in the New Testament; and can any one fail to discern a superhuman agency in the transformation wrought in the character and life of this extraordinary man? You see the bold and haughty young Pharisee, highly gifted and educated, profoundly acquainted with the Mosaic law, profoundly believing in all its requirements, and scrupulously rigid in their performance. He cannot brook the doctrine taught by the disciples of the crucified Nazarene, that the morning and evening sacrifice, and all the ordinances of the Jewish ritual, are now meaningless observances. This doctrine fills him with rage; and, breathing out threatenings and slaughter, he goes forth, armed with lawful authority, to put it down; but suddenly there is a change. The angry persecutor is found meek, gentle, submissive, sitting at the feet and receiving instruction of a humble disciple of the Crucified One. The Crucified One! Paul himself would have crucified him before, but he would die for him now. There is now nothing to his eye so glorious as this same Jesus of Nazareth whom he had persecuted. He enters upon his service. He gives up all his former hopes and prospects in life. For the love of Jesus he consents to a life of severe toil and sore privation, and at length of cruel martyrdom. But none of these things move him, neither counts he his life dear unto himself, that he might testify the gospel of the grace of God. "What things were gain to me," he says, "those I counted loss for Christ; yea, doubtless, and I count all things but loss for the excellency of the knowledge of Christ Jesus my Lord, for whom I have suffered the loss of all things, and do count them but dung that I may win Christ, and be found in him, not having mine own righteousness which is of the law, but that which is through the faith of Christ, the righteousness which is of God by faith" (Phil. iii. 7-9). How do you explain, gentlemen, a fact like this, an undoubted fact, which, however conspicuous, is far from standing alone in the annals of Christian history? Changes equally impressive abound in lives less prominent than Paul's. To countless numbers who have hated the name of Jesus, that name has become the dearest of all names, in earth or heaven. Souls burdened with a sense of sin, deeply conscious of that guilt which every thoughtful soul, wherever found, sometimes feels, have gained deliverance through their faith in him, whom they ever after love and praise, as their Life and Lord and All-sufficient Saviour. They testify to his ever-living power. Their lives, as well as their words, bear witness that this same Jesus that was crucified lives, and is able and willing to save. *Jesus saves.* HE DOES SAVE. If you doubt it, come and see. Examine the records of Christian biography with which Christian literature abounds. Take instances, which I doubt not are found in your own city. And if you say there is so much hypocrisy and deceit that you know not what or whom to trust, take the best of all courses, and test the matter by your own experience. In that sense of sin, which you, I know, sometimes have, and of whose power your Hindu records furnish such copious and such impressive illustrations, — a sense which continually deepens in the thoughtful soul, while the fact which it discloses becomes more dark and terrible the more profoundly it is considered, — Jesus Christ offers to save you; and you have the surest way to test his truth and strength, by making application of his word.

4. Jesus Christ never fails to satisfy the soul that trusts him. "If any man thirst, let him come unto me and drink," he said; and a great multitude, whom no man can number, have hied to the fountain, and found joy and peace in its

living streams. It has been a source of comfort and strength, alike to the profoundest and the simplest understanding. It satisfied the great soul of Chalmers; and it satisfied the poor and ignorant woman who applied to him for admission to the Church, and who could only tell him what she thought of Christ in these words: "I cannot describe him, but I would die for him." Lofty and low, learned and ignorant, have alike found in the gospel all they could hope or desire. Its gifts are unrestricted by any land. They come to all people. It offers the richest blessings, freely, to any heart that will receive them; and no one who has actually tested it has found the offer vain.

Whether Christianity be divine or not, that which it has actually done merits for it the most earnest attention of every man. A religion which can go about among the poor and lowly and uneducated, and which can gladden and strengthen and purify them wherever it goes, and which at the same time can feed and fill and satisfy the lofty intellects which, in every age, have bowed to its power, may have in it something which every man needs, and into which every man surely should inquire.

I do not suppose that any fair examination of the evidences of the Christian religion ever led to their rejection. Such an examination has never been given by those most prominent in their denial of this faith; for their utterances indicate either an ignorance of its character and claims, or a prejudice against them, — states of mind which show that a fair examination has not been made. Two men of fine intellect and thorough scholarship, but disbelievers in Christianity, once set themselves to write treatises for its overthrow. They took each a distinct theme; but each became converted to the Christian faith by the investigations which his theme required. They wrote their treatises, which we still have, — Gilbert West's "Observations on the Resurrection of Christ," and Lord Lyttleton's "Observations on the Conversion of St. Paul," and which illustrate what I suppose would always follow a thorough examination of Christianity, even by an unbeliever. I might instance Neander, the great church historian, born a Jew, and converted from Judaism because he saw that the evidence of the gospel was irrefutable; or Coleridge and Schelling, who have exercised so potent an influence upon the currents of philosophic thought, and who, starting with an entire unbelief in Christianity, were compelled to accept it by the requirements of the profoundest speculation; but enough already appears to force the conviction that Christianity not only ought to be examined by every man, but that its examination is the most important work which any man who doubts it can possibly undertake.

Gentlemen, if Christianity be true, two things are also true : you are saved by it, and you are lost without it; and these are also true of every human soul. If Christianity be true, Jesus Christ can save, and he is the only Saviour. If this system has truly come from God, then God has so loved the world that he gave his only-begotten Son, that whosoever believeth in him should not perish, but have everlasting life : and then also is there salvation in no other; for there is none other name given under heaven among men, whereby we can be saved. Is there any other question, therefore, so momentous to you as this? any other upon which your eternal life or death hinges? Remember that this question is not, whether Christianity is the best of all religions, but whether it is the only religion which is truly good. It claims to be the only scheme of salvation. It claims to be God's method; and God's method must be one and single. Am I not, then, justified in saying that no question relating to power or enjoyment, or even your bodily life, — no question that can be named, — has such interest for you, such undying interest, as the question whether it is true that Jesus Christ is the Son of God and Saviour of the world?

III.

THE LIGHT OF LIFE.

GENTLEMEN, — On the walls of the famous lighthouse of Eddystone is the inscription, "To give light and to save life." It tells the reason why the lighthouse stands there. The benighted mariner, approaching the Cornwall coast at a point of peculiar peril, beholds the beacon, and escapes the danger. Twice since a lighthouse was first erected there, has it been destroyed; and the wrecks of costly vessels, and the loss of precious lives, which, in each instance, ensued, furnish copious testimony to its value. No one doubts, that, by giving light, it is also the means of saving life. He who in full sight of the danger would still press heedlessly upon it, would be a madman.

Now, reasoning from analogy, it is very easy to argue, that, if there were only some spiritual lighthouse disclosing the perils of the soul, the voyager of life would steer his course with safety; but the analogy does not hold. In the spiritual world life is not saved by light: spiritual perils are not avoided, even though they are seen. If light were sufficient for safety, there would really be no danger of this sort; for spiritual light shines unceasingly and everywhere. The light of the natural sun, filling the heavens and flooding the earth, is but the symbol of that effulgence which fills the moral world with a brightness outshining the sun. The proof of this is seen in the striking uniformity in the opinions of men respecting moral truth and obligation. People the most diverse and remote, with the most extraordinary differences of government and religion and social usages, are yet agreed upon the foundation questions of right and duty. Such men as Epictetus and Marcus Aurelius and Seneca and Socrates and Shakya-Muni and Zoroaster and Confucius show that the light of duty is original and universal in human nature, shining with different degrees of clearness, but in every man sufficiently to show him where his safety lies. Whether these rays of light are so uniform because the shinings of one divine Sun, or what their explanation, I do not now inquire. I only wish to point to their universal prevalence, and to make prominent the truth, that they belong to a man just as his manhood does, and are as essential to him, and as inseparable from him, as is his human nature itself.

But we cannot contemplate this fact without meeting also another, equally prominent and universal. Clear as is the light, undoubted as is the voice of duty, men do not follow it. In this I only state a matter of actual fact, apparent to yourselves and to every one. Is it not true, that men in general do not live up to their moral convictions? I do not care to ask or argue the question whether there are any exceptions to this rule; for it suffices if you acknowledge that there are some men who do not do what they know they ought to do. And is it not indisputably true, that great multitudes, to say the least, are justly liable to this charge? Can you name any virtue upon which men have not turned their backs, in defiance of light not only, but also of entreaty and expostulation? And is there any vice or crime or sin, in the long catalogue of transgression, which men have not actually chosen and continued in, notwithstanding they saw the wrong which would thus be done, and the ruin which would thus ensue? The voyager of life has a chart on which his course is clearly traced. Every peril is distinctly noted. Lighthouses stand along every dangerous coast. Beacons blaze from every cliff. He has a compass which never varies, and the stars are shining where there is no sun; but all this will not keep him from destruction. He will steer upon the shoals, and be wrecked upon the breakers, notwithstanding all his light and warnings; for he has done it, and is doing it still. Who has not read of such instances in the past, and who does not see them all around him at the present day? And this, we should remember, is not simply the case with unlettered men, but is even more conspicuously true respecting persons of culture, in whom the light shines clearest and farthest. Who are the monsters of vice and crime, staining the bloody pages of past history with the darkest dye, and exceeding the prevailing wickedness of their time by the depth of their own corruption, or who to-day are the men upon whom your eye fixes as the chief foes to law and liberty and social order, but those whose clearness of intelligence has only made their iniquity more clear? It was a Roman poet, and a pagan, who uttered what every far-seeing observer echoes: "I see and approve the better, but I follow the worse."

It is thus apparent that the trouble with human nature relates to the inner source and centre of a man's moral purposes and moral life.

It is not the intellect, but the will, which is at fault. I make no inquiry here about the origin of this state of things. I simply deal with actual facts, respecting which there can be no dispute. However originating, there is actually found, in the human will, a deep perverseness, which the human intellect is abundantly able to disclose, but not in the least able to destroy. If we do not like this fact, it still remains inexorably true; and if we shut our eyes upon it, thinking thus it is not there, this is only as the ostrich thrusts his head in the bushes, and deems himself unseen by the hunter because prevented from seeing him. The fact itself cannot long be ignored. The conviction of a prevailing lack of harmony between our moral conduct and our moral insight is too clear and too prominent to be hid. It forces itself to view, and no one can see it unmoved to pain. Call it by whatever name, — a sense of wrong or guilt or sin, — it carries with it a consciousness of blameworthiness which contains both shame and fear, and is the source of the deepest misery the soul ever experiences. No torture of the rack or the stake has equalled the agony which men have found in the conviction that they are not what they ought to be. Against this conviction arguments are futile. To say that it is a phantasm of a morbid consciousness meets the undoubted fact, that it grows with the increasing knowledge of ourselves, and that it is not confined to the weak and ignorant, but is sometimes found with the strongest force in the strongest minds. To suppose it occasioned by certain peculiarities of endowment or early discipline contradicts its exhibition by persons of the most diverse traits, and of exactly opposite training. It is not confined to Christian lands; but instances are not wanting among the unchristian nations, where the consciousness of guilt has uttered itself in terms absolutely appalling. Some of the most startling and pathetic examples of this consciousness are furnished by your own Hindu records. The truth is, that, wherever any clear insight into the actual condition of human nature prevails, a blameworthiness, with its attendant fear and shame, appears; and we can neither ignore its presence nor destroy its power.

You will agree with me, gentlemen, that a remedy for this condition would be an incalculable blessing. If there could be something to destroy this prevailing wretchedness by drying up its source, — which could relieve from the sense of evil by removing the evil itself, — would not this be the greatest boon which human nature could either receive or desire? Surely no region ravaged by a pestilence, and crowded thick with the dying and the dead, ever needed relief so perishingly, as the world, with its undying consciousness of sin, — more destructive and more fruitful of misery than any mortal malady, — needs salvation. Do you not in this agree with me? Does not the world itself, through all its systems of religion, express the same?

It is clear, that if any true salvation be found, it must reach the will, and not stop short with any processes of the intellect. A man's intellect would be well enough, if his will did not lead him astray; but his deceived heart turns him aside, and instils his intellect with falsehood, notwithstanding its witness to the truth. There is something exceedingly subtle in these processes of the human mind, which, if we are wise, we shall not overlook. It has become a proverb that —

> "A man convinced against his will
> Is of the same opinion still."

Men are generally unconscious, till they prove themselves, of the net-work of sophistries which the will weaves around the intellect. It is not uncommon for persons to learn that they have been strangely deceived, and that they held fast to some false doctrine even while they thought they were holding to the truth; and when some clear truth, with overpowering conviction, has penetrated and dispelled all delusions, and has poured its light in such full effulgence upon the intellect that the will was no longer able to cloak it, men have sometimes found that their will has not yielded to the truth, but has turned away from it in hatred, or set itself against it in rage. I am not dealing now with speculations, gentlemen, but with undoubted facts of human nature, of which some of you may have been conscious, and which all of you, as close observers, must have seen. The actual fact is before us, — the darkest, saddest, and most terrible fact which can be named, — that, when the will is no longer able to blind the intellect, it still can and does refuse to yield to the truth; it can and does set itself in opposition to the truth; and the truth, thus, which has deeply convinced, does not save. The plant looks upwards spontaneously, and welcomes the sunlight which is to weave from its tissues its perfection of beauty. The animal runs without constraint to his food, and rejoices in the sustenance which is to give him the completeness of his strength. But the human soul, needing a perfect conformity to the truth for its beauty and strength, more than any natural thing needs its natural support, is able to pervert, and attempts to poison, the very source of its purity and health. There can be no possible remedy for this which does not, besides convincing the intellect, also convert the will. Any salvation for man which can bring true health and gladness and purity of soul must possess, not simply a means of instruction, but have also power of inspiration. It must be able to furnish to the will a new principle of life and liberty.

But a deeply-interesting question here arises, How could such a remedy ever be found? If the true remedy must work upon the will, what sort of elements, to enable it thus to do, must it possess? "Mere intellect," said the lynx-eyed Aristotle, "mere intellect never moves any thing;" while it is not only movement, but a movement in exact counteraction of another already existing, that men must have in order to be saved. Whence such a movement? Plainly from no increasing light of duty. In a French story, popular not long ago, there is a scene in which an escaped convict finds himself in a crowded courtroom, where his own crime has been charged upon another person then on trial for the same. It is a case of mistaken identity; but the evidence is clear, and the unfortunate prisoner is likely to be condemned. The real offender, unknown to any one present, but fully conscious of the mistake which has been made, and the wrong which is likely to follow, is conscious also that he ought to prevent the wrong by acknowledging himself to be the criminal. We are then treated to an elaborately-drawn process of argumentation, which the guilty man is supposed to hold with himself, to determine whether he shall do what his convictions of duty demand. The result of the process is his coming forward, and declaring to the astonished court that the prisoner ought to be released, while he himself should rightfully take his place. Such a scene may do for a French novel; but it is not high art, and does not reveal the great artist, because it is not true to actual life. Such a result could never be reached in such a way. The moment a man begins to argue with himself whether he will do his duty, he has already secretly settled it in his will that the duty shall not be done; and, unless something other than his argument comes in as a motive, the end of it all will find him exactly where he stood at the beginning. No man does his duty simply from the knowledge of it. "Knowledge," said one, who in far reaching insight was Aristotle's peer, "knowledge puffeth up, but charity — love, the living root of freedom — buildeth up."* Unless a man loves righteousness, no knowledge can make him righteous. Love alone has strength to lead one to duty; but love is not an inference. You reach it by no process of argument. You do not even choose to love. Love inspires your choice, and is not its object. Love enters the will with a living inspiration, and makes one willing in the day of its power.

From all this it follows that no self-renovation is possible. The enslaved will cannot emancipate itself. We need the power of another will to be exercised upon our own. It is quite clear, if closely scanned, that nothing can work upon a will but a will itself, or something into which a will enters. A thought may instruct us; but we can only be inspired by a person, or a sentiment or deed which comes from, and carries with it, a living personal agency. It is not light which saves us, but only life. It is not the precepts of life, but life itself, which alone can lead and lift us into life. As in the world of organic existence, life is only begotten and nourished by life; so in the moral and spiritual realm, all deep sentiments, all great deeds, are evoked and nourished by something kindred to themselves. The first

---

* 1 Cor. viii. 1.

incitement and only support to any personal activity come from what is itself personal.

If there be, therefore, any salvation for men, it must, first of all and last of all, possess this element of personal power; it must be able to enter the soul with a true inspiration, delivering the enslaved will from its bondage, and giving it the joy of a true liberty by infusing it with the strength of a perfect life. And it can only do this by presenting before us, in a form we can apprehend, a living person, whose sentiments and deeds can truly inspire us, whose will can become truly dominant over our will, and who thus becomes truly our King and Lord, to whom we yield, and whom we follow in the joy of our new-found freedom, and with the full strength of our new-found life. Would not the knowledge of such a person be most desirable? If there could be found a teacher who is also a saviour, — one who could both instruct us in duty and inspire us to a living obedience, might it not be claimed for him that he should receive the homage of the world?

To these facts add another equally clear. Among all the personages of history, only One has ever proposed for himself such a work; and only in behalf of One has it ever been claimed that he has actually accomplished it. There have been many great teachers, to whose doctrines we yield our assent, and to whose lives we give our admiration; but only One among them all claims to be a saviour. To a world dying for want of a living, personal saviour, only One living person has offered himself as all that the world needs. You know to whom I refer. You anticipate me when I say that Jesus Christ alone, through all the ages, claims to be a saviour for men. He is indeed a teacher. He stands conspicuous; he stands peerless among all the sages of the world. You yourselves will acknowledge his pre-eminence here. But not on this account, not simply because He is the greatest of teachers, does he claim the allegiance of mankind. The greatness of Jesus Christ is in his offer of salvation and his fitness to save.

Any heroic deed carries with it some power of inspiration. Any act of self-forgetfulness or self-devotion has a tendency to kindle in other souls the same. Love begets love. But as all the light and warmth in the natural world come, through various transmutations, only from the sun; so every loving and self-forgetting deed has its source, through whatever medium transmitted, in some shining of God's love. In him alone is the fulness of love. From him alone can all love spring; and only in the clear manifestation of him and his love, in a form easy to discern and impossible to deny, is there an exhaustless energy of inspiration sufficient to overcome all self-seeking, and to kindle every selfish will with the life and liberty of self-forgetting love. But such a manifestation requires the personal appearance of God, in a living embodiment of himself among men. Only thus can we most truly and fully receive the inspiration of his love.

Theism speaks of God as a living spirit, to whom human souls may come and worship; but it presents no living motive thus to do. Much as we might wish it otherwise, the lamentable fact remains, that men do not spontaneously come to God. Left to themselves, they seek their own ends, and turn away from him. Simple theism has nothing to reverse this tendency. Its thought of God is too vague to have personal power over men. As the sunlight, all glorious though it be, does not warm the atmosphere through which it passes till its beams have been reflected from the earth; so the light of the knowledge of God may shine resplendent through all our thoughts, without any vivifying warmth, till our thoughts receive it through some living reflection of him. Herein is the fitness of Jesus Christ to inspire and save men. He appears before us as the living God in human form. It is claimed of him that he is the eternal Word, which was in the beginning with God, and which was God; by whom all things were made, and without whom there was not any thing made that was made.* He repeatedly makes the same claim for himself.† He supports this claim by his own words not only, but by a power over Nature which bore witness to his words. He showed himself to be the Lord of things created; and thus he manifested forth his glory, and his disciples believed on him.‡ Nature appears as his servant, which hears his voice, and does his will. He turns the water into wine. He speaks to the winds and waves, and they obey him. The trees of the field, and the fish of the sea, do his bidding. He heals diseases of every sort. He makes the blind to see, and the deaf to hear, and the dead to live. Through the three years in which his public life was manifested, Nature is seen to move as responsive to his will as the pulse beats with the throbbing of the heart; and, when he was crucified, dead, and buried, he rose from the sepulchre, as the Lord of life, with power over death and

---

* John i.

† Matt. ix. 5, 6; xi. 27; xviii. 20; xxvi. 64; xxviii. 20. Mark ii. 9, 10. Luke v. 23, 24. John v. 19, 20, 23; viii. 58; ix. 36, 37; x. 15, 30, 38; xiv. 9, 13, 14; xv. 23; xvi. 15; xvii. 10, 21.

‡ John ii.

the grave. These facts are supported by so many and such competent witnesses, that an unwilling world has been forced to accept them; and they stand out in the face of the most searching scrutiny ever directed towards any facts, with an evidence unrefuted because irrefutable.

The significance of these facts is in the evidence they furnish that the Creator and Lord of Nature is man's Redeemer. God is manifest in the flesh, that he might reconcile the world unto himself. In Jesus Christ, God comes nigh to man, in order to lift him from his degradation and sin unto the purity and the blessedness of a divine fellowship. This is not because of man's repentance or propitiation, or good works of any sort, but solely because God loves him, and seeks to save him. God commendeth his love to us, in that, while we were yet sinners, i.e., before we had purchased his favor by any act of obedience, Christ died for us.* Here is not only a work of God's free grace; but whoever thinks carefully will see that in no other imaginable way could God's love to man be made known. It is very clear that this love is revealed through none of the processes of Nature. Not only have men failed to find it there, — all religions from

---

* Rom. v. 8.

the light of Nature giving no glimpse of God's grace, — but Nature cannot give man any such revelation, simply because Nature has not got it to give. Nature reveals the Divine Existence. The things made declare their Maker. Nature gives vast proof of God's power and wisdom. The earth and the heavens are resplendent with these glories. Nature also teaches us his beneficent goodness. The infinite adaptations of created things to living wants, and the boundless provision of Nature for our sentient need, are everywhere recognized, and are fitted to awaken universal praise. So, also, when we look widely into the course of history, and see the working of a supreme Ruler, who putteth down kings and setteth up kings, who enlargeth the nations and straiteneth them again, we find witness of a divine righteousness and justice, to which the human conscience also clearly responds. But in all this there is no evidence that God loves man, or that he can forgive sin. His beneficent gifts, doubtless, show that he desires our happiness; but they contain no revelation of his love. These gifts are but the products of his will. They cost him nothing. He has but to speak, and they are done. But love is the leaving of one's self for another: love is the giving of one's self to another. God's love to man cannot be shown in any gifts of his creation, however rich and numerous. It is the bestowal of himself, the gift of his uncreated fulness to needy souls, which alone can bring any revelation of his love. Moreover, the gift truly expressive of love must cost the giver something. Love is a sacred and sacrificial fire, which can burn only on an altar; and God's love, when profoundly considered, is inseparable from the thought of a sacrifice. God's incarnation, and the manifestation of himself to us in the person and life and death of Jesus Christ, is a sacrifice from whose mysterious depths comes a declaration of grace and love which Nature had no voice to utter, and which man himself had otherwise no power to discern.

This love of God, thus revealed, has a power to inspire men; and the light of the knowledge of the glory of God, in the face of Jesus Christ, is also life to the world. For, let one grasp the full significance of the statement; let him truly see that the work which men have vainly sought to accomplish by their sacrifices and rites, God has wrought by the gift of himself in the person of his Son; let it clearly appear that God has done all this for men, not because they deserved it, but only because he loved them; not because he needed them, but because they stood in such perishing need of him; not because he should be enriched by the returning allegiance which his love should enkindle, but only that they might be endowed with his unspeakable fulness: let it but be known that God so loved the world that he gave his only-begotten Son, that whosoever believeth in him should not perish, but have everlasting life,* — and there is a power in this love which enters the will with a living inspiration, and kindles there a love, which shall render obedience in liberty to the law of righteousness. He who can stand against all the revelations of law, who has resisted every commandment, and refused obedience, must yield to the power of the love of the Son of God. Does not love always seek and secure its counterpart? Is it not thus even with human love? I have only to know, that, among human hearts, there is one which loves me, and though I have scorned and hated and bitterly entreated it, yet its love shall melt me, and bring me to penitence and gratitude and love. In like manner, if I can truly see that God loves me, and has given himself in Jesus Christ to me, — as truly and as fully to me as though I stood alone in the great immensity, the only object of his care and grace, — whatever has been my attitude towards himself and his

* John iii. 16.

law hitherto, this knowledge of his love becomes eternal life in whomsoever it is received.

I have heard of an artist who wished to make a statue of Christ. The idea filled his soul; but, before attempting to express it in marble, he sought to mould it in clay. To test his work, he set the clay image upon a pedestal, and summoned his little child to behold it. There was no inscription upon the image; none of the ordinary accompaniments belonging to the representations of Christ — no cross, no crown of thorns — were there; but so perfectly had the artist represented his ideal in the clay form, that it is said the child, as she gazed upon it, reverently folded her hands, and exclaimed, " The Redeemer!" In like manner, I believe that the portraiture of Jesus Christ and his work, as given in the New Testament, needs only to be contemplated by the childlike heart ready to receive its impressions, and there will come to the soul a revelation of the divine love, which carries its own witness to its truth, and which is able to change any soul, however selfish, into the likeness of God's love. The life of Jesus Christ has a light which is also the life of men.

IV.

THE NEED OF A DIVINE WORK IN MAN'S REDEMPTION.

Gentlemen, — The universal prevalence of a religious sentiment has been often remarked. "Go over the world," says Plutarch, "and you may find cities without walls, without theatres, without money, without art; but a city without a temple or an altar, or some order of worship, no man ever saw." There is, almost everywhere, connected with this sentiment, the conviction that God has revealed himself unto men in some special way, in accordance with which alone a union with him becomes possible. So deep and wide-spread is this conviction, that attempts to ignore it, or explain it away, have always failed; while the authors of these attempts have sometimes borne unwitting testimony to the power of this conviction, even upon themselves. Lord Herbert of Cherbury, who has been called the prince of English deists, in his autobiography, published by his family some years after his death, relates, that having written his book, in which he had sought to set aside the notion of a divine revelation, and being in doubt as to the propriety of its publication, he knelt before his open window, and prayed the Supreme Ruler to resolve his doubts by an audible sign from heaven. He goes on to declare, that the answer was actually received; and on the strength of the sign, which he supposed to be a revelation from God, he publishes his book, in which he seeks to show that any other revelation from God than that which the original light of nature furnishes is both unnecessary and impossible. Lord Herbert pens the account, apparently unconscious of the singular contradiction of his act to his doctrine; but the account illustrates how ineradicable is the conviction that men need a divine revelation, and that, in some way, the need can be supplied.

And yet I meet the question very frequently among yourselves, whether men have not sufficient light of their own, and whether they need any other way than their own repentance to gain access to God. What need of a book and a mediator? you say. Cannot we find God, and approach unto him, directly of ourselves? Such a question is doubtless worth consideration; and yet, if you closely note it, you will see that the very terms of the inquiry furnish its sufficient reply. For who are *we?* and who is *God?* and how can the finite find the Absolute? or how can we approach him? The truth is, the finite only finds itself through the Absolute, and we only gain our own self-consciousness through our consciousness of God; for the partial, the incomplete, has no power of self-revelation. The partial is never disclosed save in the presence of the Perfect, — the incomplete in the light of the All-complete. As there is no standard of the ugly, the false, and the wrong; as these can only be measured and manifested by the beautiful, the true, and the good, — thus also the finite cannot limit itself, and cannot make itself known even as finite. It is brought to light, it is seen to be, only in the presence of the Infinite. We therefore have no being nor power to find God, save as he first finds us, and discloses ourselves to ourselves in the light of his presence.

This point, correctly apprehended, is destructive of a notion current among yourselves that our self-consciousness, inasmuch as it recognizes the self as other than God, is the very sum and substance of our sins. This surely cannot be, if our consciousness of self is only possible through our consciousness of God. Our personal being is in this personal self-consciousness; and to call this sin obliterates all moral distinctions, and falsifies the very ground of truth itself. The fact of sin is deeper, and far different from this. Not that we are conscious of self as other than God; but that, being thus conscious, we have determined to centre the self upon itself rather than upon him, — this is the secret of our sin. We have sought self as an end, instead of God, and have thus voluntarily subjected ourselves to selfishness as our law, instead of love ; and this is the source of our shame and guilt and death. God has not made us thus; but we are the sole authors of our own sin. The self-consciousness which he gives is a reality, for it is founded in him; and it is a good, for it is fitted to find purity and blessedness and life in him. Not in our self-consciousness, but in our self-determination, is our sin; and not in the self-determination, which, abstractly considered, pertains to our freedom, and is involved in self-consciousness, but in the determination of the self, not simply by itself, but to and for itself, — a determination thus which chooses self, and prefers self, and serves self, rather than God. Sin does not consist in any limitation of our powers, of which God, in making us finite, is the wise and righteous Author, but in a direction of our powers, which, in our self-determination, we have made and chosen for ourselves. We recognize this sin as a wrong, for which we condemn ourselves, and which we know, also, to be worthy the condemnation of God. We suffer under this recognition, with a suffering as peculiar in kind as it is unequalled in degree. What consciousness does not testify to the difference between the suffering which comes from a calamity uncaused by ourselves, and that which arises from our own sin? To suffer wrong, and to do wrong; to have regret for what another has done to us, and to have remorse for what we ourselves have done, — what a broad gulf separates these two in every thoughtful mind! To seek our own self-end rather than God, to make selfishness our motive and law rather than love, is an act of folly so stupendous, that a reasonable being must see its unreasonableness; and, when one recognizes such an act and state as legitimately his own, he cannot but feel therewith the keenest sense of degradation. But the unreasonable is seen to be such, only in the light of the perfectly reasonable. It is the perfect by which alone the imperfect is measured and made manifest. God's revelation of himself is the light in which our self-consciousness becomes disclosed; and it is in the knowledge of his all-perfect holiness, that we come to know our sin. In other words, sin becomes revealed to us, as contrary to God's will; and the clearer view we have of him, the more abhorrent to him does sin appear, and the more degrading to ourselves. It is his will, as revealed in the original light of our self-consciousness, that we should love him. Such a command is both wise and righteous, and calls for both our obedience and praise. It is the highest privilege, and the source of our only blessedness, to love God. To turn away from him, and make ourselves our centre, is the turning from life, and the choosing of death. Selfishness is our curse and woe, though we have chosen it for our delight. This is no arbitrary arrangement; for it only becomes manifest to us in the light of the Eternal Reason. We see it to be divinely reasonable and just that selfishness should blight every hope and destroy all joy. Self-seeking must ever be self-destructive, for life is only in love. We speak truly when we say that God has ordained it thus; but he has ordained it only because he saw its reasonableness, — only because it was worthy of him, as Eternal Reason, thus to do. Whatever is reasonable must ever be his will, not because any nature of things makes it so, nor because the reasonable is some external necessity which constrains his will, but because God himself is the Absolute Reason. It is, therefore, most reasonaable for the finite reason to love and worship God. He is our rightful Lord. He is the universal Sovereign; and all the reasonable relations of things are ordained of his almighty and eternal will. The law which we should have obeyed, but have broken, — the law of love, — is a divine law. The consequences of obedience or disobedience are divinely assigned. That the selfishness which is our sin is a curse to us, the greatest curse we can conceive; that it brings with it ruin and every woe, — is a divine decree, which only expresses divine wisdom and all-perfect righteousness; a truth which, when profoundly considered, becomes exceedingly terrible. Divine wisdom does not change; divine righteousness is eternal. Is there, then, no change for the curse of sin? Must these consequences of death and ruin be perpetual?

Explain it as we may, this question has actually excited more earnest thought, and the answer to it awakened a darker terror, than any other inquiry that has ever engaged the human mind. Neither the light of nature around us, nor the original revelation of God within, has been sufficient to indicate a reply of abiding peace. How inexorable is law, and how certain the penalty of transgression, as revealed in nature! Throughout the natural world, no violation of law ever escapes its punishment. No skill nor industry, no compromise nor subterfuge, can, in the least, avail for a refuge. The broken law vindicates its majesty, and shows its power, in the exactest punishment. Why may it not be thus also in the spiritual world? Is there any thing in Nature to teach us otherwise?

Neither can we gain any different result from the light within. We know, from this light, that the penalty of the holy law we have broken offers no escape without some justifying reason; but whence can such a reason come? Can we furnish it? Our repentance for the past, and our perfect obedience for the future, give, of course, no justification of our previous wrongdoing; but can they give us any hope of God's forgiveness? Is it reasonable for him to forgive sin because of any thing which the sinner can do? Have we any original knowledge of him which contains the probability, or even the possibility, of this? Certainly, if such a reason exists, it must be ultimately in him. The only motive to himself must ever be himself. It can never be, therefore, because of our repentance or good deeds, that he forgives us, but only because he finds it worthy of himself thus to do. But who shall tell us that it is thus worthy? He has already told us that sin is worthy of punishment. All the light of his holiness bears witness, in the original insight of our consciences, to this. When we bring him, therefore, our oblations, — our penitence and prayers and purposes of obedience, — what evidence have we that he accepts the offering, and bids us go in peace? His justice may never be set aside: he is, and must be, the eternally Just and Holy One; but when the justice of punishment is so conspicuously revealed, how can we discern the justice of pardon? How is it possible for God to be just, while he justifies the sinner?

I believe the person who ponders this inquiry most profoundly, with no other light than his reason originally possesses, will hesitate longest before propounding any other answer than that which Nature constantly gives respecting the violation of her laws. Punishment is the eternally reasonable merit of sin, and God must be eternally reasonable. How, then, can punishment fail? Arbitrarily to exchange punishment for pardon is unreasonable, and thus impossible for God. The exchange, if made at all, must be for a reason, all-sufficient to himself; and what can this be but himself? Only for his own sake, because of his infinite excellence alone, would it be right for him to pardon; but it is in his infinite excellence that the demand of punishment is grounded. He punishes for his own sake, because he abideth faithful, and cannot deny himself. Because he is the righteous Lord, he loveth righteousness, and must ever hate iniquity. I venture to say, that, with the knowledge which God has already revealed to us respecting punishment, no knowledge of pardon would be possible except through some new revelation from him. This revelation he could doubtless make through his spiritual communications directly to each soul, just as he can reveal the sunlight through the twilight of the morning, before the sun has appeared; but, if it shall be clear and full and unmistakable, it will be given in a sensible form, like the full rising of the sun, to which all men can appeal, and in which the simplest and the feeblest understanding, alike with the strongest, may find inspiration and hope. I believe you will agree with me in this, and that here is the basis of the sentiment so universal, that men need a revelation from God which their senses can cognize. Moreover, if God shall make known to us a way of pardon, it must be seen to be reasonable in our eyes as well as in his; otherwise, we could not believe it to be true. And as the reason satisfactory to the Divine Mind can be nought other than God himself; as God must find in himself alone his only and all-sufficient reason for pardon, — so, if pardon shall be revealed to man, the reason for it must be seen to be wholly divine. It must be altogether a divine gift. To rest it, in any degree, upon any thing human or finite, would be unreasonable. To suppose that pardon is possible, when we see that punishment is divine, would be a mockery of God, and tantalizing to man, unless we can see that the reason for pardon is also and only divine. Whether pardon is possible or not, we can easily see that our repentance cannot purchase it, and that the hopes which ground it upon any work or merit of man must be illusive.

The ground of pardon must be thus wholly in God; and, if it exist, it must be perfectly consistent with God's eternal right of punishment. But that these two can consist together is at first view inconceivable to man; they seem in exact contradiction. How can God pardon, unless he gives up his right to punish? and how can he give up a right which is itself eternal and divine, and still be God? Oh, question of all questions this! Men, in their perishing need, have sought for an answer of hope, but have found only despair. Superficial souls may hide their convictions, and banish their fears, by superficial observances, by their own repentance and offerings of devotion; but over thoughtful minds, who recognize the futility of any thing the human or the finite can do, and to whom no evidence of a divine work in their behalf appears, there settles a darkness as impenetrable as it is terrible.

But what is impossible to man is possible with God. In the Christian scheme of redemption the all-sufficient answer appears. Differing from all other answers, here God is represented as himself redeeming man from the punishment of sin.

The punishment is not set aside without a reason, without an all-sufficient reason; for God himself appears, and offers himself, in his all-perfect work, as the justifying reason for it. The Eternal Reason or Word, which was in the beginning with God, and which was God, became flesh, and dwelt among men. He enters the nature which had sinned. He becomes a living event in the history of the fallen race. He is a true man, and reveals the original capabilities of human nature in all their perfection. He is among men, and brings to light, by his witnessing presence, their infirmity and guilt. But he is God with men, truly human and truly divine. In him dwelt all the fulness of the Godhead bodily. This fulness he sought to give to needy souls. He humbled himself that he might exalt them. He who was rich became poor, that we, through his poverty, might become rich. He became obedient unto death, even the death of the cross, that he might save us from the curse of our disobedience, and procure for us eternal life. The obedience was freely rendered. The life which he offered was altogether his own. "No man taketh it from me," he says; "but I lay it down of myself. I have power to lay it down, and I have power to take it again." Was the law of love ever glorified as in the perfect obedience of this perfect man, in his life and death of love? What an attractive power in this obedience! what a mighty influence it is fitted to have upon selfish hearts, wherever it could be made known, — drawing them from their selfishness to love!

But what has this to do with pardon? Reformation of life will not remove the defilement of guilt already incurred. We need something more than new incentives to obedience, however desirable these may be. Moreover these, however mighty, would be powerless to move us to action, unless there were something also to inspire us with the hope of pardon. Does the perfect obedience of Jesus Christ give us any such hope? Does the offering of his life in the sacrifice of a perfect self-abnegation, wherein he fulfilled the divinest requirement, furnish any ground for pardon?

Remember that Jesus Christ, as truly man as any one of us, bone of our bone and flesh of our flesh, is also truly God over all, blessed forever, the eternal Creator and Ruler of all things. It is a divine obedience, therefore, which we have to contemplate here. He who became thus obedient to the perfect law is himself the almighty Sovereign. It was his right to reign. It behooved him to be Lawgiver and Lord through all his worlds. In the perfection of his sovereignty over his creatures was their perfection and blessedness. The river of the water of their life could proceed, clear as crystal, only from his throne. When he becomes a subject, therefore, though it is a human obedience which is rendered, it is also infinitely more than this. It has a divine significance and worth and glory. It possesses a merit thus which no finite obedience could possess. In the offering of Jesus Christ, in completest self-abnegation, there is revealed to us a divine offering, a divine sacrifice, which divine justice may not have required, but which divine love is all able to accomplish. Justice may not have required it, but what may not it require of justice? When we say that the offering is divine, have we any other terms wherein to measure its merit than to say that it is exhaustless? And when the Son of God, having finished his work, and come off as a conqueror, and more than a conqueror, demands the pardon of sin, — demands it of justice, — is this any thing more than justice must grant? In the immeasurable merits of his priceless obedience and self-sacrifice, God can be just, and yet justify the believer in Jesus. For his own sake thus he pardons, even as it is for his own sake he punishes. In the inscrutable mystery of his wisdom, and in the infinite all-sufficiency of his love, he has revealed to us a divine harmony of grace and justice, wherein mercy and truth have met together, and righteousness and peace have kissed each other.

You ask me, gentlemen, for the proof of all this, — a proper inquiry; but before answering it, let me remind you, that, if it is true, it is not only an all-perfect provision for pardon, but it is the only perfect provision that has ever been proposed. Examine other religions, and, at the best, they offer only some finite ground as the reason of pardon. At the best, it is only the merits of men which they propose as the means of obtaining the divine favor. If they ever present us, as some of them do, with theories and histories of divine incarnations, they never hold up these as the meritorious ground of pardon. Repentance, sacrifices, good works of men, are all that any of these religions offer as the object of faith or the ground of hope; but for the sake of these, can it be expected that God will remit punishment and pardon sin? What are these, at the best, when judged by infinite righteousness? At the best, do they reach farther than duty? Are they more than ought to be done? What reason, therefore, can they offer why failures in duty should be forgiven? There is not one of these systems of religion which will bear the scrutiny of an honest thought. There is not a believer in one of them who does not convict himself of a groundless faith the moment it is examined. But whether Christianity be actually true or not, you must acknowledge that its provision of pardon is ideally perfect; its ground for forgiving sin accords with perfect righteousness; it meets all the requirements of justice, and all the needs of man; and, among all the religions of the world, it is the only one not defective on both these points.

That the Christian religion is actually true, as well as ideally perfect, has one grand proof. The resurrection of Jesus Christ from the dead is the irrefragable confirmation of all that he taught and suffered. He came as a Saviour. The Son of man is come, he said, to seek and to save that which was lost. He had declared that the life which he offered up was given as a ransom or redemption for men (Matt. xx. 28). Through the shedding of his blood, he had taught his disciples, was to come the remission of sins (Matt. xxvi. 28). He had claimed, that, to himself, belonged upon earth the power to forgive sin, a power acknowledged as belonging to God alone (Luke v. 20–26). He had repeatedly declared that eternal life for men came through him, and through him alone (John iii. 4–18; v. 21–24; vi. 40–47). These claims are attested and made valid for men everywhere, in all ages, through his resurrection from the dead. If he actually died upon the cross, and was buried, and rose again from the tomb, as is claimed, this is a divine seal upon his work, which manifests its all-sufficiency in the divine eye, and which enables it to be proclaimed as glad-tidings of great joy to all people. The central evidence of the Christian system is precisely here. Wise as are the words of Christ, mighty as are his works, grand as his life seems, and sublime as was his death, the all-sufficient evidence that he is the true Redeemer and Life of the world, through whom and through whom alone forgiveness of sins can be obtained, fails without his resurrection. The ultimate proof of it all hinges here. This is the central and cardinal doctrine of the Christian faith, without which there is no such faith. If Christ be not risen, said Paul, then is our preaching vain (1 Cor. xv.). I cease, gentlemen, all my solicitations that you accept Jesus as your Lord and Saviour, unless it be literally true that he rose from the dead; but if this be true, then the Christian religion stands before you, not at all as a suppliant, imploring your assent, but as a sovereign which commands the allegiance of the world, and must compel it also.

The historical evidence for this fact is singularly convincing. I believe that any one who studies it for the first time will be surprised at its fulness and clearness. The disciples of Christ were not expecting any such event. What he had told them beforehand respecting his death and resurrection they had either imperfectly understood, or had wholly perverted. They were saturated with the prevailing Jewish notion, that the Messiah, or Christ, when he came, should be a temporal prince, actually and visibly restoring the kingdom of David. They were not prepared for his death, much less for his resurrection. The first announcement that he had actually risen seemed like an idle tale to the disciples, and they believed it not (Luke xxiv.

11). After he had really appeared to them, and they with united voice had told the fact to one of their number not present at the time, so incredulous was he, that he declared he could not believe it without the most indubitable proof to his own senses. "Except I shall see in his hands the print of the nails, and put my finger into the print of the nails, and thrust my hand into his side, I will not believe" (John xx. 25). These doubts of the disciples are very significant to us. They prevent our doubts. They show us that the important fact we are summoned to believe was sufficiently scrutinized by those most competent to judge of its truth.

Notwithstanding these obstinate doubts, the disciples all became convinced. They received such palpable proof that their Master had risen from the dead, that every doubt was dispelled. Then followed a most wonderful revolution in their views respecting him, and in the whole procedure of their life. Few and feeble as they were, and cast down through his death, they received in the forty days after his death a hope and courage and strength with which they faced the world, whose submission they demanded to their Lord. They rose now to a new view of his kingdom. They entered into the meaning of his death. They saw the fulness and power and glory of his redemption; and they preached repentance, and remission of sins through his name. This revolution in their thoughts and life they ascribe to the evidence they had received of Christ's resurrection, through which they declare they do not hesitate to preach him as the Saviour of the world (Acts ii. 24–32, iii., iv. 8–13, x., xiii.; Rom. x. 9; 1 Cor. xv. 5–20; 1 Pet. i. 21).

Now, that the disciples can have been mistaken respecting so palpable a fact is both incredible and inconceivable. They knew well the personal appearance of Jesus, and could not have been imposed upon by any false representations, even if we could conceive of such having been attempted. Nothing surely could have made them believe that they had seen and felt and handled the living body of their Master after his death; that they had heard his voice, and that he had eaten before them, to convince them that they saw not a mere shadowy representation of him; and that these appearances had been given at different times to numbers of men and women, singly and collectively, — unless there was a reality in the resurrection which put it beyond a doubt. They were not easily convinced, as we have seen; and, if they really believed what they so unanimously came to affirm, it can only have been because their affirmations were true.

Did they not believe it? They could not have been deceived themselves; but did they try to deceive the world? This is equally incredible. For what motive to such a course? What hope could they have of success? Was not the sepulchre in which the dead body of Jesus was laid, sealed, and a Roman guard set to watch it? and could not the story of his resurrection be falsified in a moment if it was not true? Were not the Jews who had plotted his death, and the Romans who had permitted it, ready enough to dispute such a fact unless it had been indisputable? But the disciples declare it everywhere. They make it the basis of their preaching. They hold it up as the irrefutable evidence of their doctrine, in the very city where the event is declared to have taken place, and among the people who had every opportunity to test the fact, and from whom innumerable witnesses could have proved its falsity if it had not been true. And the proof is clear beyond all denial, that the resurrection of Christ was believed in Jerusalem itself, by thousands who had seen his crucifixion, and who, by the irresistible evidence of his resurrection, were led to believe in him as their divine Lord and only Saviour.

Moreover, the disciples gave every evidence of being credible men. They speak soberly, as of the things which they have both seen and heard. They are not men likely to be led away by their fancies. They are plain, matter-of-fact, though so earnest men. They give every appearance of truthfulness. They are evidently seeking no selfish end. Their whole life, after they have begun to preach the resurrection, shows the highest forgetfulness of self, and an absorbing devotion to the good of others. When Christ was apprehended they were terror-stricken, and they all forsook him and fled. When he was put to death they were dismayed. But there was never a bolder set of men than these same timid disciples, after they began to speak of their Master's resurrection. In defence of this doctrine they met opposition and persecution, and faced death itself without shrinking. They laid down their lives, rather than give up the doctrine which they preached. There is no explanation of their conduct unless their doctrine was true.

The historical truth of the resurrection of Christ has never been impugned. The witnesses for it are sufficiently numerous and sufficiently credible to compel any candid assent. It falsifies every element of human nature, and contradicts every principle of historical criticism, to suppose that the disciples were either deceivers or deceived. The statements and the conduct of these men render each of these suppositions equally impossible. The doctrine which they taught must be true; and therefore God's seal is set to the great truth of Christ's redemption, who was truly delivered for our offences, and raised again for our justification, and who is the propitiation for our sins, and not for ours only, but also for the sins of the whole world.

Gentlemen, there can be but one living and true God, the Creator and Ruler of all things. It is against him that the whole human family have sinned. By his original communications to every soul, he has revealed the fact of sin and of punishment. All races of men, in every age, bear true and terrible witness to this. If, in these original communications, there is also seen any way of relief from sin and its just doom, you will acknowledge, that, at the best, the vision is exceedingly faint, and the wide-reaching conviction that it needs to be enlarged by an additional revelation testifies to its inadequacy; but if in any soul there be any sense, however faint, that God can forgive sin, it is clear that he can do this only for his own sake. The reason for forgiveness must be satisfactory to himself, and can be thus only himself. The way of pardon can be only the one which he provides; and this implies that there can be only one such way. God's method must be the best, and thus, single. If he forgives and purifies in any case, it must be for the same reason that he would in every case. Diversities of religion, different ways of pardon and of a divine fellowship, are intrinsically impossible. It is as absurd to suppose that there can be different religions, equally valid, as that there could be different sciences equally true. Science, so far as it relates to the same facts, is single. To suppose that different people have different sciences of the same objects is to suppose that some of them at least are holding to sciences falsely so called. What would you say of me if I should hold up a system of mathematics as suitable for me and my race, but having no significance for you? Would you not tell me that any science is worthless for one unless it be valid for all? And what shall I say of you if you turn aside from Christianity as being well enough for Christians, while you cling to your Hinduism as the religion separately adapted to you? Does not the fact that you talk of this religion as yours, and as separately adapted to the Hindus, show that it is not adapted even to yourselves, and that you yourselves have no profound conviction of its truth? You make no effort to propagate your faith. You send no missionaries abroad. You do not believe that your religion has any application to any other portion of the human family than your own. Therefore, I say, you have no right to believe that it has any beneficent application to yourselves; and, in your heart of hearts, you do not and can not believe it. The very fact, that, as a religion, it is not fitted for all, proves that it is not fitted for any. I call upon you to accept a religion which has no narrow claims. The Christian religion does not admit for itself any limited application. It demands universal acceptance. It does not allow that its method of salvation is one out of a number from which men may safely choose. It claims to be the only way. It holds itself up unfalteringly as the religion for every nation and every soul. Its ideal position is perfect. It offers pardon, not upon partial or finite grounds, but through a provision of which God himself is the all-sufficient author and finisher. That the perfect obedience of the Son of God to the broken law, accomplished in the incarnation and life and death of Jesus Christ, opens a way for pardon acceptable to God, is put beyond a question through Christ's resurrection from the dead. Here is a religion, therefore, which has all the elements of universality and perpetuity. Do you wonder that it does not decay, nor grow old nor weak nor weary? Do you wonder that it goes on, steadily subduing the nations? Do you wonder that you are called upon to accept this faith, and yield your wills to Jesus Christ as your Lord and Saviour?

MIRACLES.

I TAKE up this book which we call the Bible; and, whether or not I acknowledge its truth, I must at least confess its power. No other book has moved the world as this has done. I inquire into the secret of this, to discover which I am obliged to open the book to see what it contains; and I find in it really but one thought, — a thought, indeed, of incomparable grandeur and of innumerable relations, but which, itself, is as single as it is sublime. All through the Bible, I discover only what is involved in the great thought of redemption. Man's need of redemption, and God's copious provision for it, furnish the wonderful theme of this wonderful book.

Somehow or other, the Bible has convinced men that this thought is true; and it cannot be doubted that here is the secret of its otherwise inexplicable power. Men have been persuaded that an all-sufficient redemption has been freely provided by a sovereign and gracious act of God himself; and the book which contains this announcement, and furnishes the evidence of its truth, is, therefore, glad tidings of great joy unto all people who receive it. Men prize it, and embrace it, and mould their lives according to its precepts, because convinced that its story of redeeming love is true.

What has wrought this conviction? There are two ways in which we become convinced of the truth of any thing, and only two. In one, our minds behold the truth in its own light. The truth is then self-evident, and convinces us by the simple manifestation of itself. We express this conviction when we say that we know a statement to be true. Knowledge is this immediate beholding of the truth; and, when we profess it, we rest in it with an unshaken conviction.

But there are many truths of which we are convinced, but which we do not thus immediately see, and which we cannot be thus said to know. We are convinced that there is such a city as Peking, though we perhaps never saw it; we have no doubt that water is composed of oxygen and hydrogen, though quite likely we never made the experiment, and saw the truth for ourselves; we are confident that the differential calculus has solved vast and intricate questions in science, and that the method of quaternions is able to solve many more, though very possibly not one of these problems has ever been worked out by ourselves. These truths we accept, not because we behold them in their own light, but because they are affirmed by the competent testimony of those who have thus beheld them. We express this conviction when we say that we believe a statement to be true.

Knowledge and belief do not differ in that the one is a stronger conviction than the other. The conviction may be just as strong of the truth we believe as of that which we know. We may be no less certain of the existence of Peking, which we, perhaps, never saw, than we are of the existence of Boston, which we, perhaps, see every day. The difference does not relate at all to the strength of the conviction, but wholly to the kind of evidence on which the conviction rests. In knowledge, this evidence is the light of the truth itself as it becomes directly disclosed to the mind; in belief, the evidence is the testimony of another.

A belief may become changed into knowledge. I may believe certain truths of science because scientific men relate them, and I may come to know these same truths through my own experiment or demonstration. The human mind has ever an impulse to know that in which it has believed. The belief is the stepping-stone and the constant stimulus to the increasing knowledge.

In like manner, the knowledge becomes the ground-work of a growing faith. The finite mind can never know all things. Though the sphere of its knowledge be constantly enlarging, the sphere of the unknown appears to grow in an equal degree; as, with a candle in a dark place, the farther the light reaches, the greater the surrounding darkness seems. There will be always, therefore, something for us to believe. We shall always need a voice to come to us out of the darkness, and tell us of the unknown.

Knowledge and belief may be indefinitely blended; but they are the basis of all our convictions. When, therefore, the Bible convinces us of its truth, it must be, either because the truth is known by us in its own light, or because we believe it on the testimony which declares it. Now, as a matter of fact, we find that the conviction which the Bible does induce is a belief in its truth. It does not come before us, like a book of geometry, with its theorems all demonstrated, so that every principle which it utters may be revealed in its own light to our knowledge; but it is chiefly a system of faith. It appeals to our belief. Its prime evidence is the testimony of another.

But what sort of testimony is necessary to secure our belief? When one affirms to us a statement which is beyond our knowledge, we believe it just as far, and just as strongly, as we know that he who affirms it is too wise to be mistaken, and too honest to deceive. If we know the perfect wisdom and perfect truthfulness of a person, we believe his word with as strong a conviction as that of any knowledge. The belief always implies some sort of knowledge to rest upon, — some acquaintance with the truth declared, or with him by whom it is declared; but it conveys to us truths which our knowledge at the time when we received them has no means of reaching.

Now, the knowledge of God is the primal and constant knowledge of any soul. "To know God," says Jacobi, "and to possess reason, are one and the same thing, — just as not to know God, and be a brute, are the same thing." This knowledge may be vague and indefinite and obscure in many instances; yet, in every instance, is it the original possession and inalienable substance of the human mind: so that, as Cicero says, "There is no one of all men so savage, that his mind is not tinctured by it;" and, as the Jew Philo says, "He who possesses this knowledge is a man, and he who is destitute of it is no man."

We know that God is, and that he is all-wise, and cannot lie; and the Bible assumes this knowledge, and rests all its statements upon it, expecting us to receive them because they come from God, whom we know to be so wise that he cannot be mistaken, and so truthful that he will never deceive. Of course, if this foundation is secure, whatever is built upon it must surely stand. If we can only be convinced that God has spoken to us, we can no more doubt the word thus spoken than could the earth have maintained its formlessness and darkness when the Spirit of God brooded over the abyss, and God said, "Let there be light."

The whole question, therefore, hinges exactly here: What is the evidence that God has spoken? How shall we be convinced that the Bible is his word? The question is not, "How shall God flash conviction upon the mind by some self-evidencing statement?" but, "How shall he reveal his own testimony to the truth? Manifestly, this can only be through some directly spiritual and internal communication, or through some outward and sensible disclosure of God's presence. But a communication wholly internal, while it might be sufficient for the person to whom it is immediately given, would have no power to convince another, and would be liable to the same difficulties as attach to a conviction secured through external and sensible means. These, therefore, must be the methods employed. If God shall ever seek to convince us of the truth by his testimony to it, he will manifest his testimony in a way which the bodily senses can perceive. But this is only to say that he will do it by miracles; for a miracle is nothing more nor less than a manifestation, through the senses, of God's testimony to the truth. A miracle is a sensible event, wrought by God in attestation of the truth. It, therefore, must occur in Nature, and require for its production that which Nature does not possess. It must occur in Nature, otherwise it would not be apprehensible to our senses; and it must, at the same time, be beyond the power of Nature to produce, otherwise it would not disclose an agency which belongs to the Author of Nature alone. A miracle is not simply an extraordinary event, like an eclipse or an earthquake, which, however unfrequent, occurs through the regular action of the same forces that produce the ordinary events in Nature, and which might be foreknown by one acquainted with its cause; but it is an event which Nature, by its own action, never would have brought forth, and for which the power of God alone is adequate. It is no new birth from Nature's teeming womb, but a new beginning, which rises at once from an almighty fiat. It is not a development, but a creation. It is an absolutely new force introduced into Nature, by which Nature is checked and changed. The simplest definition we can give, therefore, of a miracle, is a counteraction of Nature by the Author of Nature.

Whether such counteractions have ever been wrought; whether this vast and intricate mechanism, the exquisite adjustments and delicate interdependence of all whose parts fill us with unceasing wonder, has ever been changed in any of its workings by a power outside itself, — is the grave and difficult question we must next consider.

In seeking the answer to this inquiry, let us ask, in the first place, whether there can be a sufficient occasion for such an interference with Nature as a miracle implies. Is such an interference needed to give us any further knowledge of God than Nature discloses? Are not the invisible things of him, from the creation of the world, clearly seen, being understood by the things that are made, so that men are without excuse? and do we need any thing more? We need nothing more, certainly, to convince us of our obligation and responsibility; for such a conviction all men possess. But, in the actual condition of human nature, what a terrible conviction this is! To know that we ought to do right, and that we have done wrong, and that we are responsible for this to a tribunal of infinite justice, is a knowledge in which the human soul has found an irrepressible and yet unutterable agony. If we fancy that this is the result of some dreadful delusion, and would disappear if all men could only come to see that there is no such thing as unmixed ill, and that "evil is only good in the making;" and that their so-called sin is only a phase of their imperfect development, which advancing thought and culture are sufficient to remove, — we must at least admit that such a fancy contradicts the deepest and most universal convictions of mankind, which we may well be hopeless of attempting in any such way to eradicate. The conviction of sin as a dark and terrible reality occupies a place in the actual human experience, of which it refuses to be dispossessed by any process of argument. The difference between suffering wrong and doing wrong, between the regret for what another has done to us and the remorse for what we our selves have done, is a difference which no dialectics can make to disappear, and which the common consciousness of mankind recognizes as a gulf broad and impassable forever. No subtle discriminations nor attempted subterfuges have long cloaked or crowded down this conviction; but it has disclosed itself, through every contrivance to conceal it, as the deepest source of woe which the human soul possesses. No torture of the rack or the stake has equalled the agony which men have actually experienced from the consciousness of sin.

This suffering can only be removed by removing the sin in which it has its source. But how is this possible? To stop sinning causes neither the sin nor the suffering to cease. It is not simply a theory of human nature which justifies this assertion, but the actual facts of human experience, — the darkest, saddest, and yet the most undeniable facts of our history. It is a simple truth of common experience, that a soul conscious of its transgressions does not lose that consciousness by any act of subsequent obedience. The consciousness of sin, however vaguely it may appear in some minds, always discloses a violated divine authority, whose requirements of justice and retribution the understanding and the will can neither stifle nor satisfy. If there be any relief from the misery of sin, it can only come from this violated authority itself; but no knowledge of God which the soul originally possesses, nor any which Nature can furnish, is sufficient to suggest even the possibility of any such relief. Nature adds to that of the human conscience her own testimony of the heinousness of sin. She tells us of the righteousness of punishment, and the inexorableness of law; but, in the myriad voices with which she speaks of duty and of God, there is no intimation of forgiveness or of love. That God is good, in the sense of desiring the happiness of his creatures, Nature abundantly discloses: but that he can do more than confer upon them the benefits of creation, satisfying one created object by another; that he has a heart which pities, and is willing to pardon, and which yearns to communicate himself — his uncreated and divine fulness — to needy souls, the heavens which declare his glory, and the firmament which showeth his handiwork, the day unto day which uttereth speech, and the night unto night which showeth knowledge of him, nowhere disclose. If God's mercy to sinners be a truth, it is a truth, not of Nature, but of a supernatural world; and it reaches heights of glory in the supernatural which the human intellect has, of itself, no power to ascend.

And the evidence of this, if the proof were wanting, is found in the fact, that the soul, with no other instruction than itself or Nature can furnish, has never attained such knowledge. In all the records of paganism, while the divine power and wisdom and justice, and even beneficence, are clearly declared, no mention is made of the divine love. In the idolatrous sacrifices, in the penances and prayers, of the heathen, there is doubtless indicated some vague idea of propitiation, — some undefined conviction, that, in some such way, God may be approached and pleased. But that God is a being who approaches us before we make any attempt to draw nigh unto him; that he regards us in mercy because of his love, and not for the sake of our good deeds; that he is a God who pardoneth iniquity because he delighteth in mercy, — would seem to be a thought which the natural heart, uninstructed by any special divine revelation, is unable to attain.

I confess, therefore, to a kind of surprise, when I find certain scholars and cultivated writers of our own time and neighborhood classifying the Bible with the Koran, and the Vedas, and the Zendavesta, and the Five Volumes, to which Confucius and the Chinese appeal. Such a classification, considered simply as a matter of literary criticism, is very superficial, and is creditable neither to the discrimination nor the culture of the writers who make it. The Bible, certainly, stands alone, and immeasurably distant from all other books, in this one grand characteristic, — that its religion is the religion where God is yearning and seeking after man, and where man is invited and entreated and commanded to draw nigh unto God, solely on the ground that God has already come nigh unto man. That God takes the first step in religion, that he begins the work of human restoration and deliverance, nowhere appears till the Christian Scriptures have announced it. What grand and awful visions of divine justice did the old Greek dramatists behold! What terrors of righteousness and retribution have been heard, in cries of anguish or groans of despair, all over the world! But who has known that God is gracious, that he can forgive sin, that he loves man, until the Bible has first made the blessed announcement?

But if this thought, which is the single and peculiar theme of the Bible, be true, can any thing be so important to man as its communication in a manner which shall show its truth to be indisputable? And if Nature cannot declare it, and the human mind alone cannot reach it, how is this communication possible, unless directly announced by God himself? And how shall this announcement be proved to be from God, unless he shall irrefutably manifest himself in connection with the utterance? And how can this manifestation be, except through that miraculous interference with Nature already described? If God's mercy to sinners be true, and if this truth shall ever be declared to those who are perishing for lack of it, we may expect the declaration through a miracle.

And now we are to notice, that, while the Bible announces this great doctrine of redemption as true, declaring that God has provided a perfect remedy for sin, it also claims to be a miraculous revelation. It professes to prove the doctrine by miracles which furnish God's testimony to its truth. In both the Old Testament and the New, miracles are continually adduced as a motive for faith. The Lord accompanied the call of Moses to deliver his people with a miracle; and, when the faith of the chosen leader was thus elicited and confirmed, miracles were wrought, whose express design, as stated by the Lord himself, was to attest to the children of Israel the divine commission with which Moses was furnished: "That they may believe that the Lord God of their fathers, the God of Abraham, the

God of Isaac, and the God of Jacob, hath appeared unto thee."*

Miracles were still further wrought, not only to establish the faith of the Israelites, but to convince the Egyptians themselves: " And the Egyptians shall know that I am the Lord, when I stretch forth mine hand upon Egypt, and bring out the children of Israel from among them." †

After the Israelites had been delivered by miracles, and their faith still staggered, miracles were continued for its confirmation. In announcing these before they took place, Moses says, " Then ye shall know that the Lord hath brought you out from the land of Egypt." ‡

When Korah, Dathan, and Abiram rebelled, a signal miracle was wrought in special attestation of the divine commission of Moses. The design of the miracle Moses declares, when he says, " Hereby ye shall know that the Lord hath sent me to do all these works; for I have not done them of mine own mind." §

When Moses had died, miracles bore witness to the divine authority with which Joshua was invested: "And the Lord said unto Joshua, This day will I begin to magnify thee in the sight of

---

* Exod. iv. 5 ; cf. 8, 9.   † Exod. vii. 5 ; cf. ib. ix. 29, and xi. 7.
‡ Exod. xvi. 6 ; cf. 7, 8, 12.   § Num. xvi. 8.

all Israel, that they may know, that as I was with Moses, so I will be with thee."*

When the people of Israel had forsaken the worship of Jehovah, and had gone after the priests of Baal, they were brought back to their former faith by a miracle: "The God that answereth by fire," said Elijah upon Mount Carmel, "let him be God." "Then the fire of the Lord fell, and consumed the burnt-sacrifice, and the wood, and the stones, and the dust, and licked up the water that was in the trench. And when all the people saw it they fell upon their faces; and they said, The Lord he is the God, the Lord he is the God."†

A prime motive of the miracles of Christ was to convince those who beheld them of his divine authority. When John sent two of his disciples to Christ to say unto him, "Art thou he that should come, or do we look for another? Jesus answered, and said unto them, Go and show John again those things which ye do hear and see, — the blind receive their sight, and the lame walk, the lepers are cleansed, and the deaf hear, the dead are raised up, and the poor have the gospel preached to them."‡ Before healing the sick of the palsy, he says to those around, "But

---

* Josh. iii. 7; cf. 10–13.   † 1 Kings xviii. 24, 38, 39.
‡ Matt. xi. 3–5.

that ye may know that the Son of man hath power on earth to forgive sins (he saith to the sick of the palsy), I say unto thee, Arise, and take up thy bed, and go thy way into thine house."* At the raising of Lazarus, "Jesus lifted up his eyes, and said, Father, I thank thee that thou hast heard me. And I knew that thou hearest me always; but, because of the people which stand by, I said it, that they may believe that thou hast sent me."† John bore witness unto the truth: but Jesus says, "I have greater witness than that of John; for the works which the Father hath given me to finish, the same works that I do, bear witness of me, that the Father hath sent me."‡ "If I do not the works of my Father, believe me not; but if I do, though ye believe not me, believe the works; that ye may know and believe that the Father is in me, and I in him."§ A recent writer says, "It does not appear that Jesus aimed to force conviction by miracles;"‖ but in simple fact, whether we take his own words for it, or the actual impression that his miracles gave, this is the very thing at which he was aiming. "And many of the people believed on him, and said, When Christ cometh, will he do more miracles than these

---

* Mark ii. 10, 11.   † John xi. 41, 42.   ‡ John v. 36.
§ John x. 37, 38.   ‖ Hedge, Reason in Religion, p. 264.

which this man hath done?"* In other words, could the true Messiah attest his claims in any stronger way? "Now, when he was in Jerusalem, at the passover, in the feast-day, many believed in his name when they saw the miracles which he did." † "Rabbi," said Nicodemus, "we know that thou art a teacher come from God; for no man can do these miracles that thou doest, except God be with him." ‡

The power to work miracles was given to the apostles; and they exercised it also as the proof of their divine commission: "They went forth and preached everywhere, the Lord working with them, and confirming the word with signs following;" § "God also bearing them witness, both with signs and wonders, and with divers miracles, and gifts of the Holy Ghost, according to his own will." ‖ Though the miracles may have ceased, they are recorded, that those who did not see them may also find in them a source of faith: "These are written that ye might believe that Jesus is the Christ, the Son of God; and that, believing, ye might have life through his name." ¶

We must admit, therefore, that the Bible grounds its claim to our acceptance as a revela-

---

* John vii. 31. † John ii. 23. ‡ John iii. 2.
§ Mark xvi. 20. ‖ Heb. ii. 4. ¶ John xx. 31.

tion from God upon its miraculous evidence. And as we have seen that this book stands alone in its theme, so we should also notice that it is also and equally peculiar in its miraculous claims. No other book claiming to be a divine revelation has professed to rest upon miracles. In the Koran, Mohammed expressly affirms that God's word to him is, "Thou art commissioned to be a preacher only, and not a worker of miracles."* Various threats and promises are uttered in the Koran to unbelievers and believers; but the motive to faith is declared to lie exclusively in the revelation itself.† Centuries after the death of Mohammed, miracles were related of him; but there is no evidence that he made any pretension to the power of performing them.

Many have a vague notion, that the claim to work miracles belongs to every rude age, and has been urged in support of every superstition; but this is not true. Unnumbered systems of paganism have, indeed, their unnumbered prodigies and signs and miracles; but the systems do not depend upon these. They nowhere profess to do so: on the other hand, the miracles hang upon them. Instead of giving any support to the system to which they belong, they receive

---

* Koran, Sura, xiii. 8.
† Ibid., vi. 33, 34 i x. 20; xiii. 28, 31, 38.

all their support from it. Nowhere are they presented as the evidence of a doctrine; but they come forth as the result or appendage of a doctrine already believed. The Bible, however, does not undertake so much to prove its miracles by its doctrines; but it seeks to prove its doctrines, in the first place, by them. Whether or not this claim be valid, it is at least unique.

We cannot, therefore, exaggerate the importance of miracles in the Christian system. Our belief in that system depends, at last, upon its miraculous evidence. If miracles are impossible or incredible, or cannot be actually proved, then is the Christian system a delusion. The incarnation of Christ, if it ever took place, was a miracle, without which our belief in redemption is impossible. The resurrection of Christ, if it did occur, was certainly a miracle of a stupendous sort: "But if Christ be not risen, then is our preaching vain, and your faith is also vain." *

Thus far, I take it, neither our facts can be ignored, nor the deductions from them disputed. Here is the fact of sin, and the burden of universal sorrow beneath which it buries men. Here is the need of pardon and purity, which Nature cannot give, which man cannot procure, which

---

* 1 Cor. xv. 14.

God alone can furnish, and whose announcement he alone can make through means which shall irrefutably disclose his presence. Here is the Bible, which stands alone among all books in its declaration of God's mercy, and in its adducing of miracles to prove that its declarations are from God, and are therefore true. All this is quite remarkable; but the question still remains, whether the Bible actually gives us evidence enough that its miracles did occur. The occasion was momentous: the need was incalculable. Was the occasion met? Is the need supplied?

To this inquiry the answer is, that, if the miracles did occur, no evidence of the fact could be better than that which we actually possess. No events in history have a wider and more unequivocal testimony than have these. The miracles were not done in a corner. There was no effort to conceal them. They challenged scrutiny. Though always wrought in proof of the one truth of redemption, they were done in many places, at many times, by different persons, to whom it was given to declare different points or applications of the great theme. They were witnessed by thousands. They were of such a nature, that the beholders could not be mistaken as to whether they did take place. That Christ should walk upon the water; that he should still the storm by a word; that he should raise the dead even where the body had been buried four days; that he should heal the blind, the deaf, the lame, the leper, with a touch, a look, a word; that he should be crucified, dead, and buried, and then rise from the dead, and be seen for forty days by those who had known him most intimately before his death, — can be explained by no jugglery nor deception; and these events must actually have occurred as reported, or their reporters have fabricated the stories, knowing them to be false. But why should such a fabrication be attempted? and how was it possible to carry out the deception? The apostles had nothing to gain, but every thing to lose, by such an undertaking. To affirm these stories of their Master was to bring upon them also their Master's fate. Because of their report, the apostles did suffer obloquy, persecution, and death; and, though they must have foreseen this result, they continued their declaration, ceasing not to teach and to preach that Jesus is the Christ, and that these mighty works were wrought of God through him. Does this look like an attempt to deceive? Is it possible that in all this the apostles were only acting out a lie? Surely this would be only a miracle more astounding than any which they declare.

But more than this: the word of the apostles was believed. It was believed on the very spot where the miracles were declared to have taken place, and by thousands who could have at once disproved the story if it were not true. It was believed by their enemies. The apostles furnished proof of their statements, which no amount of argument or persecution could rebut. The recital found adherents everywhere. The bigoted Jew, the scornful Greek, the proud Roman, acknowledged its force. It won its way in the largest cities of the world. It conquered the chief seats of culture. It took possession of the high places of power. Hardly three centuries from the crucifixion, a disciple of Christ sat upon the throne of the Cæsars, and the world lay at his feet. Now, as the miracles were continually put forth by the early preachers of Christianity as the evidence of its truth, it must have been believed that they occurred. But when we remember how manifest and how numerous and how marvellous the so-called miracles were, and how boldly the apostles proclaimed them, and how constantly they relied upon them, and that the numbers who participated in the scenes described, and who might have disproved the miracles if they had not occurred, must have exceeded the apostles by thousands to one, is it possible that it was all a mistake? This, I say again, would be the greatest miracle of all.

But still further: It does not appear that any one ever ventured to deny the miracles at the time when the apostles were declaring them as the reason why all the world should believe that Jesus is the Christ. Christianity did not meet with an easy reception, though it spread so rapidly. It was opposed on every hand. Persecution was not the only means employed for its overthrow. Learning and philosophy set their forces in array, and sought to demolish it on high intellectual grounds. But, in all that was said in opposition to it during its early history, not a word appears to have been uttered against the reality of its miracles. Every argument was urged which the keenest hostility could suggest; but no one seems to have thought it possible to deny that the miracles took place. But if there had been, at the time, any room for the denial, does any one doubt that it would have been uttered? We must remember that the apostles were preaching an exclusive religion. They were continually declaring that there is no other way of salvation. They set themselves against every form of doctrine, however venerable or dear, which was contrary to the name of Jesus of Nazareth; and when, in proof of their doctrine, they hold up the miracles everywhere, and no one anywhere attempts to deny them, is it not clear that the evidence for them was felt to be irrefutable?

But there is yet a stronger point. Not only did the opposers of Christianity fail to deny the miracles; they actually admitted them, and have left their testimony to the fact of their occurrence: "He casteth out devils by Beelzebub,"* said the Jewish rulers, unable to deny the fact of the wonderful work. In like manner, Celsus and Hierocles, and Julian the apostate, and the Jewish rabbis in the Talmud, — all of whom wrote and argued even bitterly against Christianity, — have yet all left their acknowledgment, which we still possess, of the actual occurrence of these events, which they seek to account for by magical arts; which Celsus affirms Christ must have learned in Egypt, and by which he was able to deceive great multitudes. Are we not entitled to say, therefore, that here is a certainty? If any thing can be certain, these facts thus reported did occur. The great doctrine which the Bible proclaims, it also proves. It is not unmeaning; it is no delusion; it is the great truth of God, that "he so loved the world, that he gave his

---

* Matt. ix. 34; Mark iii. 22; Luke xi. 15.

only-begotten Son, that whosoever believeth in him should not perish, but have everlasting life." * "Therefore we ought to give the more earnest heed to the things which we have heard, lest at any time we should let them slip. For if the word spoken by angels was steadfast, and every transgression and disobedience received a just recompense of reward, how shall we escape if we neglect so great salvation, which at the first began to be spoken by the Lord, and was confirmed unto us by them that heard him, God also bearing them witness, both with signs and wonders, and with divers miracles, and gifts of the Holy Ghost according to his own will?" †

I have thus far preferred to deal with the question on its positive side, seeking only to discover and declare the exact matter of fact, without reference to any inquiry respecting the antecedent impossibility and incredibility of these events. If it be proved — as I claim must be admitted from the evidence we possess — that miracles have actually taken place, then they are both possible and credible; and any speculative difficulties upon this point must be untenable. But, if untenable, can they not be shown to be thus on speculative grounds? and is this not de-

---

* John iii. 16.   † Heb. ii. 1-4

sirable? I answer affirmatively, and proceed, without reluctance, to the task; though, in doing this, I do not admit that the positive argument in favor of miracles needs ought further than its own statement, clearly apprehended, to compel assent.

I do not think it necessary to dwell upon the objection, considerably urged in some quarters, that a miracle is only a physical fact; and is therefore, at the best, but an argument addressed to the senses, and should not be put forth as a method of convincing the intellect. I am not sure that I understand this objection; for I cannot look upon it from any standpoint which gives it force, except as I shut my eyes to the most open facts of every man's experience. Physical facts, or arguments addressed to the senses, do continually move the intellect of every man. The sunrise is a physical fact; but does it convey nothing more to the intellect of the man who beholds it than it does to the ox? The ocean, the clouds, the stars, the human voice, the face of a friend, the form of a statue, the colors of a painting or a landscape, — all these are physical facts, — arguments addressed to the senses, if one please; but is there no beauty nor truth disclosed through them? and could the disclosure come in any other way?

Neither does it seem necessary to tarry with the objection, that a miracle indicates caprice or vacillation on the part of God. The miracle does not contradict the grand statement of Scripture, that the Lord is of one mind, and "known unto God are all his works from the foundations of the world." It may have been as truly a part of his purpose to produce the miracle as that any natural event should take place; and there is no more difficulty in supposing that something absolutely new should be introduced into Nature, than that Nature itself, as something new, should be introduced, when, "in the beginning, God created the heavens and the earth."

The first objection which I would more particularly consider has been most recently uttered by Mr. Lecky, who, in his somewhat confused "History of European Morals," deems that the Christian miracles had very little to do with the conversion of the Roman Empire, because everybody in those days believed in miracles, and no one attached any special importance to them. They were affixed to the Christian doctrine as a matter of course, just as similar wonders accompanied other recitals; but the inductive philosophy of our time has substituted a critical spirit for the credulity which then prevailed, and we are able to see that the Christian and all other miracles are equally untrue.

Now, it may be that there was a readier acceptance of the supernatural at that period than at the present time; and yet, if we subject this notion to this same critical spirit of advanced modern thought, we fail to find such evidence of its truth as the confident assertion of it would seem to imply. There were sceptics then as well as now. There were railers at the current notions of divine things, as numerous and as self-confident, then as now. There were the esoteric mysteries, not peculiar to the Greeks, but probably learned by them from the Egyptians, and found also with the Persian magi and the ancient Druids, in which the initiated were permitted to see the irrationalities of the common faith. There were Gorgias and Protagoras and Lucretius and Lucian, who would probably match any of our modern deniers of the supernatural; besides Celsus and Porphyry and Hierocles and Julian, whose earnestness of conviction no modern unbeliever in Christianity will be likely to outdo. Porphyry and Jamblichus wrote lives of Pythagoras, adorned with wonders as marvellous, to say the least, as any recorded in the Gospels; but the age was not sufficiently inclined to the supernatural to receive them with credit. Not every thing wonderful was then believed.

The truth is, that, while the supernatural may be denied by some in every age, it has always proved itself the belief of the great mass of men, and is, perhaps, as prominent at the present as at any time. Counterfeits prove not only the worth, but the currency, of the genuine coin; and the easy and wide spread of the so-called Spiritualism — not to mention other errors illustrating the same — shows that very considerable obstacles still resist the attempt to root out the supernatural from the thoughts of common men.

Now, if there was no importance attached to miracles in the days of the apostles, and if, as no one disputes, Christianity won its way in the face of every opposition, till it conquered a supreme place in the esteem of the entire civilized world, then how is this latter fact to be accounted for, unless we bring in — though the objector has no thought of introducing it — some superior intrinsic evidence in Christianity itself, by which it was able to convince the world of its truth? Men do not give up cherished convictions, and receive, instead, a doctrine which contradicts all they have previously held, for no cause. Nations do not change their customs and belief suddenly, and without any reason. Paganism, in the Roman Empire, did not die without a struggle: how came it to die at all?

It employed both persecution and argument to sustain itself: why did it not succeed? To say, as Mr. Lecky does, that it was because of a "disintegration of old religions, and a general thirst for belief," shows neither the sagacious historian nor philosopher; for the question at once recurs, How did Christianity come to satisfy this general thirst for belief? and how, in this disintegration of old religions, was the new religion able to stand, as though it was the word of God, which liveth and abideth forever? Say what we will, the indisputable fact remains, that paganism in the Roman Empire died because it was supplanted: it lost its sway because a mightier power wrenched the sceptre from its grasp; and, if historians choose to say that miracles were no element of this mightier power, then they are bound to tell us what the elements of it actually were. What is the cause of these prodigious effects? That the fruit is ripe, and ready to drop, does not explain its fall, unless there is some power of gravity to bring it down. That the nations were ready for the gospel; that Christ came, as the Scripture says, "in the fulness of time," — does not account for the conversion of the nations, unless they were convinced that he was the living object of their desire. That they were thus convinced is the indisputable fact;

but, if his miracles had no cogency, how could this have been, unless he possessed other and superior means of compelling assent to his claims? The denial that miracles had any force in the early spread of Christianity obliges one to declare that the gospel has such interior and self-evident proof, that nothing is needful but its own statements to show men that it is divine. I am willing to leave the objector undisturbed in either of these positions. Augustine long ago said, "If you do not believe the miracles, you must then believe that the world was converted without miracles; and this would be a miracle."

Another phase of this same objection relates to the test of a miracle. If we allow that miracles are possible and credible, how shall we distinguish the spurious from the genuine, — the "lying wonders," which come "with all deceivableness of unrighteousness in them that perish,"[*] and the miracles which are wrought and recorded that we might "believe that Jesus is the Christ, the Son of God"? If the magicians with their enchantments [†] did such things as Moses did, why should we not put faith in them as well as in Moses? And if Simon, the Samaritan sorcerer, [‡] was a man "to whom all of the city

[*] 2 Thess. ii. 10.   [†] Exod. vii., viii.   [‡] Acts. viii. 9, 10.

gave heed, from the least unto the greatest, saying, This man is the great power of God," why does not he have as high claims to our regard as does Peter, who denounced him to his face?

To this there is a double answer. In the first place, the Bible makes a clear distinction between the two. While it relates the wonders of the magicians and sorcerers, it also relates how these men were confounded by a mightier power than they could wield. Omnipotence is never at their control, and they are furnished with no divine attestation. On the other hand, they are continually met and controlled by what is evidently an almighty power. Still further: the Bible records certain events, which demanded, beyond dispute, God's special interposition. Such were those connected with the deliverance of the Hebrews from Egypt, by which they were constrained to say, "The Lord brought us forth out of Egypt with a mighty hand, and with an outstretched arm, and with great terribleness, and with signs and wonders.* On the basis of these miracles, Moses might appeal, as the Bible says he did, to the truth thus revealed, as the standard by which all other doctrines might be tested: "If there arise among you a prophet, or a dreamer

---

* Deut. xxvi. 8.

of dreams, and giveth thee a sign or a wonder, and the sign or the wonder come to pass whereof he spake unto thee, saying, Let us go after other gods which thou hast not known, and let us serve them, thou shalt not hearken unto the words of that prophet or that dreamer of dreams." * As though he had said, "God has given, by his miracles, indisputable proof that he is the Lord your God: let no sign nor wonder contradict this; for he never can contradict himself." In like manner, Paul, of whom Christ, after his resurrection, was seen, "as of one born out of due time," † might appeal to that resurrection as the all-sufficient voucher for the doctrines which he declared; and might say, as he did to the Galatians, "Though we, or an angel from heaven, preach any other gospel unto you than that which we have preached unto you, let him be accursed." ‡ Whether we explain the "lying wonders" as wrought by jugglery, or by bringing into play forces of Nature which only the performers knew, or by a supernatural power of evil which has been able to penetrate the natural world with its hostility to the good, — in no case does the Bible fail to furnish the means for a clear discrimination

---

* Deut. xiii. 1–3. † 1 Cor. xv. 8. ‡ Gal. i. 8.

between the two kinds of wonders which it records.

Another answer to this question will also reply to a still broader inquiry, — Why affirm the miracles of the Bible, and deny those related in other books? Are not the healing of a blind man and a cripple by Vespasian, and the print of the nails upon St. Francis, and the wonders performed at the tomb of the Abbé Paris, with unnumbered other incidents of the same sort, facts for which the testimony is clear and ample? and were not these as truly miracles as any which the Scripture records? I do not care here to scrutinize the evidence on which the reports of these marvels rest; though it must be confessed, that, in the great majority of the instances adduced, when the evidence is thoroughly sifted, it falls to the ground. But supposing we admit that a blind man was restored to sight, and a cripple to strength, by the touch and word of Vespasian, though Tacitus and Suetonius, the only authorities for the story, differ in their account to a degree, which, if found in the New-Testament writers, would assuredly be said to invalidate their testimony: but waiving this, and supposing it also to be true that the stigmata actually appeared upon the hands and feet of St. Francis, and that extraordinary cures were wrought at the tomb of the Abbé Paris, and that persons have been apparently cured of the scrofula by the touch of a king, — the evidence of any thing miraculous, or of a divine interposition for the counteraction of Nature, is still wholly lacking. The science of anthropology discloses many and curious susceptibilities to bodily changes through mental impressions; and, if these marvels happened, they may be illustrations of forces belonging wholly to Nature, and which we as yet but partially apprehend. I deny any thing miraculous in these events, and challenge the objector for his proof; but I affirm the miraculous in those great events to which the Christian Scriptures appeal, and I prove the affirmation by the occasion, the results, and the quality of the events themselves. These events took place, as we have seen, in attestation of a doctrine of incalculable importance for men to know, but whose truth no other means were adequate to disclose. They have, therefore, a sufficient occasion; while the other class has none. Give to these pagan and papal marvels undisputed evidence, and all the significance they claim, and how far does this significance reach? — simply to this, that certain marvels were done which ended with their doing; which had no results beyond the persons upon whom they were wrought; and which, so far as the pagan wonders are concerned, did not profess to have. The miracles of the New Testament were not done simply that certain individuals might be saved from certain natural misfortunes; but these natural misfortunes are removed in a supernatural way, in order that not only to these individuals, but to all the world, there may be taught the great doctrine, to wit, "that God was in Christ, reconciling the world unto himself, not imputing their trespasses unto them."* In reference to these other marvels, we may say of them, as Origen did, "What came of them? In what did they issue? Where is the society which has been founded by their help? What is there in the world's history which they have helped forward, to show that they lay deep in the mind and counsel of God? The miracles of Moses issued in a Jewish polity; those of the Lord in a Christian Church: whole nations were knit together through their help. What have your boasted Apollonius or Esculapius to show as the fruit of theirs? What traces have they left behind them?"

But the character of the events, as well as their occasion and results, determines their

* 2 Cor. v. 19.

miraculous quality. Take such instances as the raising of Lazarus or the resurrection of Christ; and to what jugglery or deception, or force of Nature, however hidden, can these events be referred? Nay, do not all our investigations of Nature, all the results of modern science, instead of pointing us to some hitherto undiscovered law of Nature as the sufficient cause of such events, put it beyond all question that no force of Nature could have produced them? Modern science has, at least, taught us that these events cannot have been natural events; and we are forced, therefore, to admit their supernatural origin, or, in spite of the evidence in their support, to deny the possibility of their occurrence.

We come, then, to this denial, in which the opposition to miracles, in our time, finds its last stronghold. A miracle, it is said, is impossible; and, therefore, no amount of testimony, nor any number of men who have believed it, can make me believe it. Nature is fixed and orderly. To change an atom would change all the worlds. To increase or diminish, in the least degree, the exact amount of forces now constituting the universe, would destroy the universe. This introduction of a new force in Nature, such as a miracle presupposes, is impossible. Forces of Nature may be dissolved, and recombined; but always their exact equivalence will remain. Nothing new can be created, and nothing old destroyed. Moreover, says the objector to the Christian Theist, you prove the existence of your Deity by an appeal to the orderly arrangement of Nature; but you can only prove your miracle by denying this same orderly arrangement. You build a stairway up to a certain landing-place, and then you maintain this landing-place by destroying the very process which led to it, and the very basis on which it stands. If your faith can rest on such a contradiction, much more may my unbelief. I justify, therefore, my denial of miracles, because they are impossible, and because the interposition of God, which they assume, demands an argument which would destroy the very proof that there is a God.

I have endeavored to state the argument fully and fairly. We should not attempt to maintain what cannot be defended against any and all attacks.

Now, it is not a reply to this objection, to say that a miracle only brings in a higher order of Nature than we had known before, and thus the miracle-worker is only he, who, knowing the event which is going to take place, but of which others are ignorant, takes advantage of his superior wisdom to secure an acknowledgment of his superior power. But this would be no miracle. It would be no communication of God to the soul. Such a view would neither maintain the Christian revelation, nor answer the objection against its miraculous evidence.

Let us meet the objection face to face, and look it in the eye. Stripped of its verbiage, it amounts to this, — a miracle is unreasonable, and therefore impossible. But what do we mean by reasonable and unreasonable? What is this supreme potency, which determines so easily whether aught be possible or impossible? The objector appeals to it most confidently; and so do we, and so do all men. What does it mean? Is it only a word without reality, and with which our thoughts cheat themselves? But, then, how idle all appeals to it must be! and how absurd this very objection becomes! If the reasonable has no reality, the objector to miracles because of their unreasonableness has no reality in the very ground-work of his objection.

But supposing we admit that the reasonable is real, and confine its reality to what an individual man perceives and judges. There is thus no universal standard of reason to which all our perceptions and judgments should conform; but the reasonable is in a man's consciousness alone, and it is unmeaning to talk of it as elsewhere or otherwise. But, if this be so, what folly to talk at all! Why should a man ever say a word if there is no universal standard of reason according to which his words can be judged by another mind as truly as his own? And how does all argument, i. e. every attempt to make others think as we do, fall to the ground, if there is not above and beyond us a standard to which we feel that not only our judgments, but those of every man, should conform! If the reasonable be only what I fancy to be so, I may not, indeed, ask the objector to miracles to relinquish his objections; but just as little may he require me to admit their force. Each man thus stands upon a ground which he can neither maintain against another, nor be forced by another to abandon; and all argument between men is vain, and all agreement among them hopeless.

But if we suppose the reasonable is something real, and has also its reality in some nature of things outside and independent of the individual mind which perceives it, we should then have a standard by which we could measure our individual judgments, and which would enable us to argue with some possibility of agreement. In this view, the reasonable would mean the facts of Nature just as we discover them. I thus go to Nature, and observe what is occurring there;

and these occurrences give me all my knowledge. I know nothing about the supernatural: the word has no meaning to me; but Nature is real, and Nature is reasonable; and this is all the reality and all the reasonableness I can know. I find no miracles in Nature, but only an invariable order, which makes the thought of a miracle absurd, and the occurrence of a miracle impossible.

Now this view, in which the unreasonable and the impossible mean only what is unnatural, deserves a close inspection, that we may see its exact quality, and to what results it leads us. If there be nothing reasonable but the facts of Nature, then, of course, nothing can be known beyond these facts; and therefore, whether beyond these, any thing be possible or impossible, we have no right to say. If the only reason for the order of Nature, as we find it, be, that we actually do thus find it, then we have no right to say that it could never be found otherwise, nor that we ourselves may not find it altogether different to-morrow from what we find it to-day. That a certain fact occurs is, in itself, no reason why it should occur again; and, if it has occurred a thousand times, this alone gives not the slightest reason for its future repetition. If we know nothing about the causes of the fact; if, as the positive philosophy stoutly affirms, we only know the facts themselves, — then to affirm any thing save what we or competent witnesses have actually observed is a most unwarranted assumption, which, if it be good natural science, is good-for-nothing logic. We have no right to generalize upon such grounds: all that we may do is to hold to the individual phenomena as we have observed them; and, if there are no miracles among these, we can say so; but to deny that miracles are found elsewhere with other phenomena is as idle as for the blind man to deny the existence of colors which he never saw, or the deaf man the harmony which he cannot hear. To talk about universal laws, and an order of Nature which requires this and requires that, is to renounce the prime postulate of the positive school; and thus these natural philosophers, who enter so confidently upon their task of mowing down and clearing up the theological thistle-field, dexterously contrive to cut off their own legs with the first movement of their scythe.

The fallacy of the objection might be illustrated, if we could suppose an observer to become acquainted with the force of gravity before there is any light or heat for him to know. Such an observer might become very conversant with Nature as then existing: he might go through the universe, and find one unvarying order binding all things to their centre; but he might not, therefore, say that any change of this order is impossible. The introduction of light is such a change. Light is the antithesis, the direct opposite, of gravity; but when the Spirit of God brooded over the waters, and God said, "Let there be light," there was light.

If we generalize at all about Nature, and deduce any thing further than the facts which have been actually observed, it is because we recognize that there is something reasonable beneath the facts, which also reaches beyond them, and which, instead of being made by the facts, has itself determined how they shall be made. The objector to miracles begins his objection by denying that there is any such reasonableness: but he is obliged to affirm it before he gets through; and thus his objection rests upon two grounds which flatly contradict each other. In other words, he denies a miracle because it is different from Nature; but he can only maintain that nothing different from Nature can be by affirming a principle which is itself different from Nature. The objector is attempting to ride two horses, which are proceeding in opposite directions, at the same time, — a feat of gymnastics not easy, certainly, for the performer, however amazing to the lookers-on. His argument is the old fallacy of the undistributed middle in the syllogism. A principle which can form the basis of a universal affirmation, and by which alone one is justified in affirming what is possible and what impossible, is not only beyond and above Nature, and must control Nature, but is recognized as such even by him who denies the supernatural; or else his denial has no more meaning, even to himself, than the chatter of a parrot or a monkey. "We must philosophize," said Aristotle; "and if one says we must not philosophize, still, in saying thus, he doth philosophize, and must do so." We must have the supernatural; and it is alike the mystery and majesty of the human soul that we cannot deny the supernatural except in terms which absolutely imply and affirm it.

We take our stand, therefore, on this position, and declare — what the very denial of it implies — that the reasonable is supernatural; and, on this ground, the objection to miracles we are now considering instantly disappears. It does not profess to have any force except as it denies the supernatural; and, if this denial fail, the objection fails at once. If there be a reasonableness which is supernatural, then there must be a supernatural Reason who has made Nature, and who is not only its Author, but its Finisher as well, beginning it and consummating it out of his own fulness, and for his own glory. Could he make it? and can he not control it? And if it be the sublime truth that God hath "created all things by Jesus Christ, to the intent that now unto the principalities and powers in heavenly places might be known by the Church the manifold wisdom of God, according to the eternal purpose which he proposed in Christ Jesus our Lord," then, what is to hinder such adjustments and interferences with the order of Nature as he may see fit to introduce for the full disclosure and accomplishment of the wondrous plan?

"To many minds," said Plato, "there must come a moral improvement before they can receive any intellectual enlightenment;" and to the minds immersed in Nature, and who boast of their inability to look beyond it, how much need there is of a spiritual insight and quickening! A man's intellect which has shut out the light of the supernatural is like a man's senses which have shut out the light of day. In either case, he walks in darkness. He speculates, perhaps; he inquires about the meaning of things; he explores Nature; he gives us his sciences, which he calls the only positive truth: but he is all the while like a blind man, who feels over with his fingers the form of a statue, or the face of a man, in order to discover thus the beauty and the living soul. Oh for the light! Oh for the opened eye! What a difference would they work at once in all his inquiries and their results! If the blind man could only see, how insignificant would all his discoveries by his fingers seem! · And, if the intellect which seeks to shut out the supernatural could only be illumined by its light, how meaningless and dead would be all its movements separate from this!

To a soul which has actually known Jesus Christ as the Saviour of sinners, and found him its light and hope of glory, and opened its eye to the lofty view which he reveals of man, of Nature, and of God, how meagre and unsatisfying seem all speculations which he has not illumined and inspired!

"THE ENTRANCE OF THY WORDS GIVETH LIGHT; IT GIVETH UNDERSTANDING UNTO THE SIMPLE. MY LIPS SHALL UTTER PRAISE WHEN THOU HAST TAUGHT ME THY STATUTES. THE LAW OF THE LORD IS PERFECT, CONVERTING THE SOUL; THE TESTIMONY OF THE LORD IS SURE, MAKING WISE THE SIMPLE; THE STATUTES OF THE LORD ARE RIGHT, REJOICING THE HEART; THE COMMANDMENT OF THE LORD IS PURE, ENLIGHTENING THE EYES."

www.ingramcontent.com/pod-product-compliance
Lightning Source LLC
Chambersburg PA
CBHW020053170426
43199CB00009B/275